UP CLOSE 4

English for Global Communication

Isobel Rainey de Diaz
Anna Uhl Chamot
Joan Baker-Gonzalez

THOMSON
™
HEINLE

Australia • Canada • Mexico • Singapore • Spain • United Kingdom • United States

THOMSON

HEINLE

Up Close, Student Book 4

Publisher, Global ELT: *Chris Wenger*
Acquisitions Editor: *Berta de Llano*
Developmental Editors: *Jean Pender, Ruth Ban*
Associate Developmental Editor: *Stephanie Schmidt*
Production Editor: *Sarah Cogliano*
Senior Marketing Managers: *Amy Mabley, Ian Martin, Francisco Lozano, Utzuinic Garcés*

Manufacturing Coordinator: *Mary Beth Hennebury*
Composition: *Graphic World*
Project Management: *Kris Swanson*
Illustration: *Ray Medici, Jane O'Conor*
Text Design: *Sue Gerould*
Cover Design: *Jim Roberts*
Printer: *Banta Company*

For permission to use material from this text or product contact us:
Tel   1-800-730-2214
Fax   1-800-730-2215
Web   www.thomsonrights.com

ISBN: 0-8384-3288-3

Photo Credits

Photos on the following pages are from PhotoDisc, Inc. Digital Imagery © copyright 2002 PhotoDisc, Inc.:

Cover (background photo; first, second, fourth on right), i (first, second, fourth on right), 2, 12, 21 (third and fourth from left), 26 (top row right, bottom row left), 30 (bottom), 32 (center), 36 (top row left), 40 (first, second, third from left), 41 (top row first second from left; bottom row), 42 (top), 47 (bottom), 62, 72, 81 (first, second from left), 85 (top row), 92 (top), 97, 112 (bottom)

Photos on the following pages are from the EyeWire Collection:

18, 21 (second from left), 26 (top row first and second from left; bottom row center), 32 (bottom), 41 (top row third from left), 81 (right), 92 (bottom), 93, 98, 102

Photos from other sources:

Page 22: Ian Cook/TimePix
Page 26, bottom right: John Luke/Index Stock Agency
Page 30, top: © Mitchell Gerber/CORBIS
Page 31, left: © CORBIS
Page 31, right: Rich Remsberg/Index Stock Imagery

Page 36, top center: Zefa Visual Media-Germany/Index Stock Imagery
Page 36, top right, bottom: © CORBIS
Page 38: AP/Wide World Photos
Page 39: AP/Wide World Photos
Page 40: fourth from left: Zefa Visual Media-Germany/Index Stock Imagery
Page 41, top row right: Image Port/Index Stock Imagery
Page 47, top: Chad Ehlers/Index Stock Imagery
Page 52: © CORBIS
Page 54: AP/Wide World Photos
Page 57, left, right: AP/Wide World Photos
Page 57, center: Reuters/TimePix
Page 60: Rick Bostick/Index Stock Imagery
Page 80: © Reuters NewMedia Inc./CORBIS
Page 82, top: © Reuters NewMedia Inc./CORBIS
Page 82, bottom: AP/Wide World Photos
Page 85, bottom left: Hoa Qui/Index Stock Imagery
Page 85, bottom right: Don Romero/Index Stock Imagery
Page 87: AP/Wide World Photos
Page 88, left: Canstock Images Inc./Index Stock Imagery
Page 88, right: AP/Wide World Photos
Page 112, top: Chip Henderson/Index Stock Imagery
Page 119, top: Chip Henderson/Index Stock Imagery

Acknowledgments

The authors and publisher would like to extend their thanks to the editorial, sales, and marketing teams in Boston, Asia, and Latin America for their invaluable comments and suggestions. In addition we would like to acknowledge the contributions of the following ELT professionals who reviewed the *Up Close* program at various stages of development and offered helpful insights and suggestions:

Ana María Batis, Instituto de Educación de Aguascalientes, México

Rudy Bedon, Asociación Peruana de Profesores de Inglés, Perú

Marlene Brenes, Universidad Autónoma de Puebla, México

Jesús Cabrera, Instituto Cultural Dominico-Americano, República Dominicana

Nancy C. Carapaica, Centro Venezolano Americano, Venezuela

Chwun-Li Chen, Shih Chien University, Taipei, Taiwan

Freda Chiang, Yang Ming University, Taipei, Taiwan

Neil Cowie, Saitama University, Urawa, Japan

Sandra Davidson, Instituto Cultural Dominico-Americano, República Dominicana

Lúcia De Aragão, União Cultural Brasil-Estados Unidos, Brasil

Rocío Domínguez, Universidad Autónoma de Baja California, México

M. Sadiq Durrani, Centro Boliviano Americano, Bolivia

Guadalupe Espinoza, Universidad del Valle de México, México

Chiu-Hua Fiu, Van Nung College, Shingzuo, Taiwan

María Eugenia Flores, Centro Cultural Costarricense Norteamericano, Costa Rica

Fernando Fleurquin, Alianza Cultural Uruguay Estados Unidos, Uruguay

Clare Gilpin, Tokyo Junshin Women's College, Tokyo, Japan

Huiya Huang, National Ilan Institute of Technology, Ilan, Taiwan

Fatma Karaaslan, ANTYK ENG & BMT, Istanbul, Turkey

Kim A Ram, Seulgee Young-o-sa, Seoul, Korea

Kim Je Jung, English Campus, Seoul, Korea

Jiny Kim, Tiny Tots Institute, Seoul, Korea

Kim So Young, Mirae Young-o-sa, Seoul, Korea

Zoe Kinney, Instituto Cultural Dominico-Americano, República Dominicana

Lee Balk Eum, English Education Center, Seoul, Korea

Lee Bo Ram, English Education Center, Seoul, Korea

Ching-Ying Lee, Kang Ning Junior College, Taipei, Taiwan

Mary Meloy-Lara, Instituto John F. Kennedy, México

Michelle Merritt, Universidad de Guadalajara, México

Carroll Moreton, Ming Chuan University, Taipei, Taiwan

Dana Parkinson, Universidad de las Americas-Puebla, México

James Riordan, Associacão Cultural Brasil Estados Unidos, Brasil

Anthony Robins, Aichi University of Education, Kariya, Japan

Maritza Rodríguez, Asociación Peruana de Profesores de Inglés, Perú

Sergio Rodríguez, Instituto Tecnológico de Sonora, México

Elizabeth Ruiz, Universidad de Sonora, México

Consuelo Sanudo, Secretária de Educación Pública, México

Judith Shaw, Kansai Gaidai University, Osaka, Japan

T. Nevin Siders, Universidad Nacional Autónoma de México, México

Kathryn Singh, Instituto Tecnologico y de Estudios Superiores de Monterrey, México

Eugenia Soto, Centro Cultural Costarricense Norteamericano, Costa Rica

Eric Ting, Kai Nan University, Tao Yuan, Taiwan

Pia María White, Universidad de Aguascalientes, México

STUDENT BOOK 4

CONTENTS

Practical Learning

How often do you...

	always (100%)	often (85%)	sometimes (30%)	occasionally (10%)	never (0%)
1. write new words in a vocabulary notebook?	☐	☐	☐	☐	☐
2. plan what you are going to say in English?	☐	☐	☐	☐	☐
3. try to use cognates to help you understand the text?	☐	☐	☐	☐	☐
4. review what you are learning?	☐	☐	☐	☐	☐
5. listen to the student CD at home?	☐	☐	☐	☐	☐

What do you like to do in English?

	always (100%)	often (85%)	sometimes (30%)	occasionally (10%)	never (0%)
1. read articles or stories	☐	☐	☐	☐	☐
2. do pair work	☐	☐	☐	☐	☐
3. perform role-plays	☐	☐	☐	☐	☐
4. write letters or e-mails	☐	☐	☐	☐	☐
5. listen to the teacher	☐	☐	☐	☐	☐
6. do grammar exercises.	☐	☐	☐	☐	☐

Outside of class, I ...

	always (100%)	often (85%)	sometimes (30%)	occasionally (10%)	never (0%)
1. watch television in English.	☐	☐	☐	☐	☐
2. study by myself.	☐	☐	☐	☐	☐
3. use the Internet to practice English.	☐	☐	☐	☐	☐
4. talk to people who speak English.	☐	☐	☐	☐	☐
5. read books and nespapers in English.	☐	☐	☐	☐	☐
6. listen to music in English.	☐	☐	☐	☐	☐

Three things I will do to become a better student:

1.
2.
3.

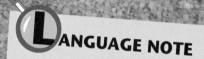

LANGUAGE NOTE

Many geographic locations are referred to by their initials:

KL	Kuala Lumpur
NYC	New York City
DC	District of Colombia
SA	South America
BA	Buenos Aires
UK	United Kingdom
USA	United States of America

Acronyms and Abbreviations help us simplify the language

NATO	North Atlantic Treaty Organization
WHO	World Health Organization
NAFTA	North American Free Trade Agreement
MS	Multiple Sclerosis
AIDS	Acquired Immune Deficiency Syndrome
ASEAN	Association of South East Asian Nations
WWF	World Wildlife Foundation
UNICEF	United Nations International Children's Emergency Fund
UNESCO	United Nations International Educational, Scientific and Cultural Organization
MSF	Medicins Sans Frontiers

PRONUNCIATION SYMBOLS

Vowels

Symbol	Key Word	Pronunciation
/ɑ/	hot	/hɑt/
	far	/fɑr/
/æ/	cat	/kæt/
/aɪ/	fine	/faɪn/
/aʊ/	house	/haʊs/
/ɛ/	bed	/bɛd/
/eɪ/	name	/neɪm/
/i/	need	/nid/
/ɪ/	sit	/sɪt/
/oʊ/	go	/goʊ/
/ʊ/	book	/bʊk/
/u/	boot	/but/
/ɔ/	dog	/dɔg/
	four	/fɔr/
/ɔɪ/	toy	/tɔɪ/
/ʌ/	cup	/kʌp/
/ɝ/	bird	/bɝd/
/ə/	about	/əˈbaʊt/
	after	/ˈæftər/

Consonants

Symbol	Key Word	Pronunciation
/b/	boy	/bɔɪ/
/d/	day	/deɪ/
/ʤ/	just	/ʤʌst/
/f/	face	/feɪs/
/g/	get	/gɛt/
/h/	hat	/hæt/
/k/	car	/kɑr/
/l/	light	/laɪt/
/m/	my	/maɪ/
/n/	nine	/naɪn/
/ŋ/	sing	/sɪŋ/
/p/	pen	/pɛn/
/r/	right	/raɪt/
/s/	see	/si/
/t/	tea	/ti/
/ʧ/	cheap	/ʧip/
/v/	vote	/voʊt/
/w/	west	/wɛst/
/y/	yes	/yɛs/
/z/	zoo	/zu/
/ð/	they	/ðeɪ/
/θ/	think	/θɪŋk/
/ʃ/	shoe	/ʃu/
/ʒ/	vision	/ˈvɪʒən/

Stress

/ˈ/	city	/ˈsɪti/

used before a syllable to show primary stress

/ˌ/	dictionary	/ˈdɪkʃəˌnɛri/

used before a syllable to show secondary stress

STRESS

Stress means to emphasize a word or a syllable.

INTONATION

Intonation means changing our tone to help the listener understand what we are saying.

STUDY UP CLOSE

Use a dictionary to check the pronunciation of words you don't know. The pronunciation of a word usually appears right after that word in a dictionary entry. In the front or back of the dictionary you will find a key to the pronunciation symbols used in that dictionary. It will be similar to the list of symbols shown here.

Coffee break

Communication	Grammar	Vocabulary	Skills
Offering choices of food, drinks, and activities	Present perfect + *just* *Would rather* + verb	Types of beverages Descriptive adjectives *Hello there!* *As a matter of fact . . .* *I've got to run.*	Listening to a talk Reading an expository text Writing a flyer
Talking about recent past events			
Expressing preferences			

1 Warm Up

A. PAIR WORK Look at the picture. Where are Julie and Mike? What are they doing? Do you drink coffee? Why, or why not?

 B. Listen. What are Julie and Mike going to order? Complete the statements below.

Julie is going to order _____.

Mike is going to order _____.

C. GROUP WORK Make a list of the most popular beverages in your country. Organize them into two groups: cold and hot. Then discuss when you like to drink each beverage. Give reasons.

2 Conversation

Coffee talk

Mike and Julie are on a coffee break. They are in a coffee shop called Café Puro. Suddenly, Mike sees Nick, an old friend.

A. Listen and practice.

Mike: So, what would you like, Julie? An espresso, a cappuccino, a café latte . . . ?

Julie: I'd rather have iced tea. The coffee here is too strong.

Mike: Okay, so it's iced tea for you. Let me see, I'll have an espresso.

Mike: Well . . . hello there!

Nick: Hi, Mike, how have you been?

Mike: Nick, I haven't seen you in ages.

Nick: I've just come back from Korea.

Mike: Korea. Wow! Come and join us.

Mike: Julie, this is Nick, an old friend. Nick, Julie. Julie has just joined us at WebWorld.

Nick: Nice to meet you, Julie.

Julie: Good to meet you, too.

Mike: What would you like, Nick? A cappuccino, an espresso . . . ?

Nick: Hot chocolate for me, please.

B. PAIR WORK Does a coffee shop serve only coffee? What other beverages might it serve? What do Julie and Nick have in common?

Mike: So how was Korea?

Nick: Great. I loved it! And where are you from, Julie?

Julie: As a matter of fact, I'm from Korea!

Nick: Really! It's a beautiful country. Wow! Look at the time! I've got to run.

Mike: I'll see you later, Nick.

Nick: Yeah, see you later. Nice meeting you, Julie.

Julie: Bye, Nick.

ⓒ ULTURE UP CLOSE

Have you ever thought about what you would need to open a coffee shop? The challenges you would face would include finding enough start-up money, planning your business, finding a great location, creating an inviting café environment, knowing how to attract customers, and above all, making an excellent cup of coffee.

GROUP WORK Name some successful coffee shops in your city or neighborhood. Do you think they did all the things suggested above?

3 Grammar in Context

Talking about recent events

Present perfect + *just*

Nick has **just** come back from Korea.	They have **just** ordered their drinks.
Julie has **just** joined the company.	Nick and Julie have **just** met for the first time.
Mike has **just** seen an old friend.	We have **just** exchanged e-mail addresses.

Has/Have + *just* + past participle tell us about recent or immediate past events or activities. This expression is less common in negative statements.

Use *recently* in questions to elicit information about recent past events.
Have you been to the pool *recently?* **No, I've been too busy.**

To elicit information about the immediate past, omit *recently*.
Have you seen Julie? Yeah, I saw her in the coffee shop a few minutes ago.

Practice

A. PAIR WORK Group the participles from the chart above under the correct heading.

Past participles: regular verbs	Past participles: irregular verbs
joined	*met*

B. GROUP WORK Brainstorm recent events and activities in your lives, and list them on the board.

Example: *Roberto and his family have just moved.*
Amanda has just started a new job.

Interact

C. PAIR WORK Using the statements in B, take turns asking and answering questions about recent events.

Example: *Have you seen Roberto recently?*
No, he's been busy. He and his family have just moved.

D. GROUP WORK Make statements about all the things you and your classmates have done in this lesson.

Example: *We have just learned about the present perfect* + just.

4 Grammar in Context

Expressing preferences

Would rather + verb

I'**d rather have** iced tea.
He'**d rather play** football.

Nick and Julie **would rather talk** about Korea.
We **would rather have** a cup of coffee.

Use **would rather** + verb in response to offers and suggestions to express other preferences.

Practice

A. PAIR WORK First, take turns offering food and drink and responding by expressing a preference for something different.

Example: a cup of tea/a cappuccino
Would you like a cup of tea?
Thanks, but I'd rather have a cappuccino.

1. some iced tea/iced coffee
2. some hot chocolate/an espresso
3. a hamburger/a chicken sandwich
4. some soup/a pizza
5. some fries/a salad

B. PAIR WORK Take turns making suggestions and responding by expressing a preference for something different.

Example: a concert this weekend/go to a club
A: *Let's go to a concert this weekend.*
B: *A concert? Well, if you don't mind, I'd rather go to a club.*

1. go for a walk this afternoon/go swimming
2. have a party this weekend/study for the tests/examinations
3. watch a movie tonight/play tennis
4. go to a French restaurant on Sunday/go to a Chinese restaurant.
5. go to Café Puro for a quick break/stay at my desk

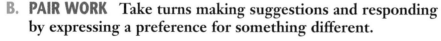

C. GROUP WORK Form groups of four. Work in pairs and write suggestions for activities to do after class. Take turns making suggestions to the other two members of your group, expressing a preference for something different, and then reporting the group's preference to your classmates.

Example: **S1:** *Let's go for coffee after class.*
            S2: *Thanks, but Carlos and I would rather go to the computer lab.*
            S1: *Okay, let's go to the computer lab./Oh, no! Not again!*

Pronunciation

LANGUAGE UP CLOSE

Use rising intonation for incomplete lists in questions or statements when offering choices or checking facts.

D. Listen and repeat.

1. What will it be? An espresso, a cappuccino, a café latte, . . . ?

2. When can we have a meeting? I can make it on Monday, Wednesday, . . .

3. Where should we go next? Tokyo, Seoul, Singapore, . . . ?

4. What would you like? A pizza, a hamburger, . . . ?

5. Where is Julie from? Korea, Japan, . . . ?

6. Do we have everything? Let's, see. Tea, coffee, milk, sugar, ...

7. Nick's an attractive guy. Tall, well-built, . . .

8. Who's going to be Julie's date? Mike, Nick, . . . ?

E. GROUP WORK Read the following dialog silently. Then, work together to draw intonation lines above the sentences. Finally, take turns reading the dialog in pairs, using the correct intonation.

A: What would you like? A milkshake, a soda, . . . ?

B: I'll have a soda, please.

C: A soda, for me, too, please. So what should we do next? Go home, go to the library, . . . ?

B: Let's go to the library.

A: What are you planning to study? English, psychology, literature, . . . ?

B: English, I think.

Interact

F. PAIR WORK You are in a coffee shop with a friend. Take turns offering each other a choice of food and drinks, and then accepting one of the choices.

Example: **A:** *What would you like? A coffee, a soda, . . . ?*
         B: *A soda for me, please.*

5 Vocabulary in Context

L ANGUAGE UP CLOSE

Use *nice and* + adjective to say that something is just the way you like it.

Describing beverages

Beverages like tea, coffee, and hot chocolate are **stimulants** because they contain caffeine.

Julie drinks a lot of iced tea on hot summer days. It's so **refreshing.**

Nick loves hot chocolate. It's very **soothing.** When Nick drinks hot chocolate, he forgets his worries.

Mike drinks a lot of coffee. He likes **strong** coffee. He doesn't like coffee that is too **weak.** He also likes his coffee **black.** He never takes it **with cream.**

Julie's favorite beverage is **black** tea, but she drinks it **weak**, not **strong.** Sometimes she drinks cappuccinos because they are **nice** and creamy.

Casey likes herbal teas. Herbal trees come from trees and plants. They aren't **stimulating.** They are **calming** because they are caffeine-free.

Practice

A. Use words or phrases from the box above to make pairs of opposites.

1. stimulating _____

2. strong _____

3. with cream _____

B. List some of the beverages people in your country drink within the following categories.

soothing beverages   refreshing beverages   stimulating beverages

Interact

C. **PAIR WORK**   From your lists in B, take turns offering one another a drink and expressing a preference for something different. Give reasons for your choices.

Example: **A:** *Would you like a lemon soda?*
B: *No, thank you. I'd rather have coffee. I need to wake up.*

A: *How do you like your coffee?*
B: *With cream, no sugar.*

 **6 Listening in Context**

Focus Strategy: **Listening to recognize main ideas and listening intensively**

 **LISTENING UP CLOSE**

When preparing to listen to a talk, it is a good idea to try to predict what you think will be said. Then, as you listen, you can see if your predictions were correct. This will make your listening easier.

Before listening

A. **PAIR WORK** You are going to hear a talk about the popularity of coffee. In pairs, check the topics you think will hear in the talk.

Before listening	First listening	Topics
		1. The names of countries where farmers grow coffee
		2. Some information about the origin of coffee
		3. The color of the coffee cups in most coffee shops
		4. Reasons why some scientists say coffee is good for you
		5. Serious diseases in coffee crops/plantations
		6. The different kinds of coffee people drink
		7. Reasons why people prefer beverages other than coffee

First listening

B. Listen for the topics. Check the boxes in A that are mentioned in the talk.

Second listening

C. Read through the incomplete notes below. Listen again and complete the notes.

Some facts and figures about coffee and coffee drinking

1. Number of coffee shops in the U.S.:	Over _____
2. One company sells:	30,000 pounds of coffee a week.
3. Some traditional coffee-growing countries:	_____; Colombia; Kenya; Indonesia, _____; Jamaica.
4. Some new coffee-exporting countries:	_____; Peru; India; _____.
5. Reasons coffee may be good for you:	Helps us _____; improves concentration; makes us more productive; _____.

Origins and history of coffee

6. People in the Near and Middle East first began to drink coffee:	_____ years ago.
7. Europeans began to drink coffee:	_____ century.

Tastes in coffee

8. Italians:	_____.
9. French:	without sugar, slightly bitter.
10. Americans and Japanese:	_____.

 **Reading**

Focus Strategy: Identifying main ideas

Before you read

A. PAIR WORK Take turns answering these questions.

1. What kind of coffee do people drink in your country?

2. What are the names of some of the most popular brands of coffee?

3. Can you describe the packaging of one of the most popular brands?

4. Look at the coffee packaging on the right. What words do you recognize? Make a list of all the words.

5. Can you guess the meaning of any words you do not know? On the back of the package, there is more information about *Feel Good* coffee. What kind of information do you think it is?

Taylors of Harrogate
Family coffee merchants. Est. 1886

Feel Good!

Organic

Great tasting coffee that gives extra help to coffee farmers.

A fresh, rich coffee suitable for all kinds of coffee makers.

 ## While you read

B. Read these headings. Then read the paragraphs and match the headings with the paragraphs.

1. It's one big family.

2. Don't panic. It's organic.

3. We give back half of the profits.

4. We pay fair prices.

_____

The families who cultivate Feel Good coffee work on small farms and cooperatives. We guarantee these farmers long-term trading agreements and the highest possible prices.

_____

The farmers who grow Feel Good do not use chemicals or insecticides on the plants or in the soil. They grow the plants in the shade and produce healthy coffee with a rich, refreshing flavor—just right for morning, noon, or night.

_____

Paying fair prices is not enough. We also share 50 percent of the profits from Feel Good with the communities that grow the coffee. We will use some of the profits from this pack to buy new furniture for the school on El Progreso coffee farm in Oaxaca, Mexico. We will use the remaining profits of that 50 percent to buy cooking stoves for families in Nicaragua. The stoves are healthier to use and are environmentally safe.

_____

Taylor's is a small family business and our staff members like to share in the Feel Good project, too. Many of our employees who work in England have offered to pack the coffee free on "Feel Good Fridays" so that even more money can go back to the farming communities.

www.feelgoodcoffee.co.uk

After you read

C. Read closely and find these facts.

1. The places where Feel Good farmers work.

2. The names of two countries where Feel Good trades.

3. Some of the people in addition to the farmers that Feel Good helps.

4. A health advantage of Feel Good coffee.

5. Where the Feel Good farmers plant their coffee.

6. The kind of company Taylors' is.

D. GROUP WORK Think about and discuss the answers to the following questions. Read both texts again if necessary and identify the sentences or parts of the text that contain the answers.

1. Why do you think the Feel Good farmers like to do business with Taylors'?

2. Why do you think there are a lot of people who like to buy Feel Good coffee? Think of as many reasons as you can.

3. Why do you think Feel Good coffee has the flavor it does?

4. Why do you think some employees are willing to work without pay on certain days?

5. Where can you get more information about Feel Good?

8 Writing

 **WRITING UP CLOSE**

Working with a partner to generate ideas makes your writing richer. After you have shared your ideas with your partner, write them using your own words.

Focus Strategy: Developing supporting ideas

Before you write

A. PAIR WORK Brainstorm with your partner to think of ideas that would convince people to buy Feel Good coffee.

Write

B. On a separate piece of paper, complete the flyer. Refer back to the text on page 8.

C. GROUP WORK Think of a project in your college, university, region, or country that you would like to support. It can be something simple, like a concert that your school choir is organizing. Write a flyer to convince more people to support the project.

D. Share your flyers with the other groups and comment on them.

Eight Reasons why you should buy **Feel Good** Coffee:

Feel Good coffee is HEALTHY. **Feel Good** farmers do not . . .
Feel Good coffee is EASY TO USE. It is suitable . . .
Feel Good coffee is DELICIOUS. It has a . . .
Feel Good coffee is EFFICIENT. You can drink it at . . .
When you buy **Feel Good**, you help SMALL . . .
Taylors, the company that markets **Feel Good** believes in . . .
Taylors also gives HALF of the **Feel Good** profits to . . .
Feel Good farmers and employees are HAPPY because . . .

Putting It Together

A. **GROUP WORK** Work in groups of three. Read the situation. Then choose and prepare one of the roles. Using your own names, act out the roles.

> **Situation:** Student 1 invites a new student (Student 2) in your class for a cup of coffee after class. A friend (Student 3) whom Student 1 has not seen for a long time comes into the coffee shop.

Role 1 Prepare to: offer Student 2 a choice of drinks; express surprise and greet Student 3 when he or she comes into the coffee shop; introduce Student 2 to Student 3; offer Student 3 a choice of drinks; ask Student 3 about his or her recent activities, and in general talk to both Students 2 and 3 in a friendly, informal way.

Role 2 Prepare to: choose from the choice of drinks Student 1 offers and express reasons for your preference; greet Student 3 when Student 1 introduces you; ask Student 3 about his or her recent activities; respond to his or her questions about where you come from and what you are doing in his or her town/city/country, and in general talk to both Students 1 and 3 in a friendly, informal way.

Role 3 Prepare to: greet Student 1 when you come into the coffee shop; accept his or her invitation to join him or her and Student 2; greet Student 2 when you are introduced to him or her; choose a drink when Student 1 offers you a choice; respond to questions from Student 1 and 2 about your recent activities; ask Student 2 about his or her origins and reasons for being in your town/city, and in general talk to both Students 1 and 2 in a friendly, informal way.

B. Change roles and act out the role-play until you have played all three roles. Remember to read your card carefully before acting out each new role.

STAY TUNED Why is Mike's boss so stressed out?

Relax or you'll burn out!

UNIT 2

Communication	Grammar	Vocabulary	Skills
Checking progress in plans, schedules, and expectations Expressing a possibility Describing emotional states	Present perfect + *so far, yet,* and *already* *May/might* + verb Word formation: compound words	Emotional states *get on someone's case* *Anything else?* *That's it.*	Listening to a radio talk show Reading a newspaper article Writing a journal entry

1 Warm Up

A. Use these words to describe how each person is feeling: *happy, down, angry, relaxed.*

 B. Listen. Use the words in A to describe each person's feelings today.

Evan is feeling _____. Daniel is feeling _____.

Carina is feeling _____. Alana is feeling _____.

C. **GROUP WORK** Make a list of common reasons why people feel down.

Example: *People often feel down when a relative gets sick.*

2 Conversation

If he doesn't relax, he'll burn out.

LANGUAGE UP CLOSE

We *get on a person's case* when he or she is not working fast enough or well enough.

Mike, Julie, their boss Greg, and his personal assistant Mel are checking the final arrangements for WebWorld's participation in an e-commerce fair in New York next week.

A. Listen and practice.

B. PAIR WORK Make a list of things they have to do for the fair. Which are still pending? Which do you think are the most important? Why?

CULTURE UP CLOSE

In industrialized countries, research has shown that many health problems are related to stress at work. Stress at work affects people in all kinds of jobs—offices, stores, hospitals, etc. In the United States, work-related stress causes bad health in 43 percent of adults. Stress at work causes a loss of thousands of millions of dollars to the U.S. economy.

GROUP WORK What do you think are the most stressful jobs in your country? Give reasons for your answers.

Greg: Let's see. What have we done so far? Have you made the hotel reservations?

Mel: Yes, I've just received the confirmation by e-mail. We're all booked for 6 nights.

Greg: Good! Mike, do we have the flyers yet?

Mike: No, not yet. The print shop says they might be ready tomorrow.

Greg: Tomorrow is too late. Why don't you give them a call back right now and get on their case. We need to have the flyers ready today.

Mike: Okay. I've been busy preparing the demos, and I still need to finish checking the website.

Greg: Well, we've all been busy lately. Julie, maybe you could help Mike see about those flyers.

Julie: Sure, Greg. I'd be happy to do that. I have a conference call in five minutes, but as soon as that's over, I'll give the print shop a call.

Greg: How about those hands-on activities for the kids? Please tell me you have them done.

Julie: They're right here!

Greg: Excellent. Is there anything else? Mel?

Mel: No, I think that's it.

Greg: Great. Thanks, everyone.

✳ ✳ ✳

Julie: Wow! Is he always so impatient?

Mike: No, but he's been pretty stressed out recently. Business is a little slow, and he's probably worried about that.

Julie: Even so, if he doesn't relax he'll burn out.

Mike: Yeah, and so will we!

3 Grammar in Context

Checking progress in plans, schedules, and expectations

Present perfect tense + *so far*, *yet*, and *already*

Have the flyers arrived **yet?**	What have they done **so far?**
No, they haven't.	They have made the hotel reservations.
Haven't they called **yet?**	Has the train **already** left?
Yes, they have.	I'm afraid it has.

Use **so far** mainly in *what* questions when checking and reporting progress in plans and schedules. **So far** comes at the end of questions and at the beginning or end of responses. It means **up to this point in time.**
So far, we have made good progress. OR **We have made good progress so far.**

Use **yet** to check what is happening with an expected action or schedule. **Yet** usually comes at the end of a *yes/no* question or negative statement.
I haven't done that yet.

Already is often used for emphasis and means **by now** or **sooner than expected.** It can come next to the expected action or event, after **have/has,** and before the past participle.
It's only 3 P.M. and I have *already* finished my work. OR **It's only 3 P.M. and I have finished my work *already*.**

Practice

A. Use *so far*, *yet*, and *already* to complete the text about the arrangements for the e-commerce fair.

Greg is checking the final arrangements for the e-commerce fair. He gets angry when he hears that the flyers haven't arrived **(1)** _____, but he is pleased when he hears that Julie has **(2)** _____ completed the hands-on activities for the kids. **(3)** _____, the team has made quite a lot of progress with their plans for the fair. For example, Mel has

(4) _____ booked the hotels, and Mike has prepared the demos. Greg doesn't seem to appreciate how hard they have all worked. He's stressed out these days because **(5)** _____ this year, business has not been good.

B. PAIR WORK First, work alone. Imagine you are going on a business trip in one week. On the list below, check the things you would have done so far in preparation for your trip.

book a hotel room

book airline tickets

search the Internet for information about the city you are going to visit

buy a tourist's guide of the city you are going to visit

prepare all your notes for the business meeting

search the Internet for information about the company you are going to visit

pack your suitcase

Clean up your desk at work

Work with your partner and check the progress he or she has made with the preparations.

Example: *Joe, have you packed your suitcase yet?*
No, not yet. I usually do that the night before the trip.

C. GROUP WORK Tell the class what you learned about your partner's preparations.

Example: *Joe has already booked his hotel room but he hasn't packed his suitcase yet.*

4 Grammar in Context

Expressing a possibility

Might/may

WebWorld **might** get some foreign business at the e-commerce fair.

The flyers **might** arrive tomorrow.

Greg **may** not be so impatient after the fair.

Julie **may** be uptight because she has so much work to do.

Mike has a sister in New York, so he **might not** stay all 6 nights in the hotel.

This use of the modal verb ***might/may*** + verb expresses that a present or future situation is a possibility, but it is not certain.

Do not use ***may*** to express possibility in questions.

Practice

A. PAIR WORK Take turns deciding what you would say in
these situations to express possibility.

Example: A friend, David, who is usually easygoing, has been under stress recently. You
are organizing a party this weekend.

David might not come. He's so stressed out these days.

OR

Let's hope David comes. It might help him relax.

1. Your class has an examination tomorrow. Alicia, a classmate, has a bad cold today.

2. The message on Julie's answering machine isn't clear. She's expecting a call from Nick.

3. There are a few dark clouds in the sky this morning.

4. You and your friends are going to the movies on Friday evening, but one of your
friends, Walt, doesn't have any extra spending money right now.

5. You are waiting for the bus, but you heard in the news that the bus drivers are
planning a strike.

Interact

B. PAIR WORK Ask and answer questions about your future.
Express uncertainty about your plans.

Example: do/finish this English course

A: *What are you going to do when you finish this English course?*
B: *I'm not sure. I might go to the United States or I might go to Canada.*

1. study/finish this English course
2. buy/begin to earn more money
3. do/classes finish today
4. eat/get home tonight
5. buy/receive your next paycheck

6. stay/visit New York
7. travel to/have enough money
8. do/have free time this weekend
9. wear/go to Pablo's party
10. live/get married

C. GROUP WORK Tell the class some of the things you
learned about your partner.

When Monica gets paid, she might
buy a CD or she might buy a book for
her history course. She's not sure.

5 Vocabulary in Context

Describing emotional states

People who never relax become **stressed out.** As a result, they sometimes **lose control** of their lives, and **can't cope** with their problems.	People who relax, exercise regularly, and do not **overwork** often feel more **in control** of their lives.	People who live to work are **addicted to** work. These people are sometimes called **workaholics.**	People who are under **stress** at work need to **relax** and try not to work too hard. If they don't, they will **burn out.**
When people are **burnt out,** they can have both emotional and physical problems. They can get **depressed** and complain of such things as headaches and backaches.	People who don't overwork and are feeling relaxed often appear **easy going.** They seem at ease with the different aspects of their lives.	On a bad day at the office, however, even an easy going person can become **uptight** or **tense.**	

 Interact

A. PAIR WORK First work alone. Think of a person you know well, and choose one of the words or expressions above to describe that person's emotional state. Make notes about the person to justify the adjective you chose. Use other words from the texts above in your notes.

Example: *Nick = very **relaxed***

> *Works hard but doesn't **overwork**   Takes regular breaks in Café Puro*
> *Walks to and from work   Sleeps 8 hours a night*

Use your notes but not the adjective to describe the person to your partner. Listen to each other and try to identify the adjective for the emotional state your partner describes.

B. GROUP WORK Explain the underlined compound words in the following sentences.

1. When Kazusa went to the mall yesterday, she <u>overspent</u>.

2. Scott <u>overslept</u> this morning. That's why he was late for class today.

3. I'm sleepy. I need a coffee. I <u>overate</u> at lunchtime.

4. Please don't <u>overheat</u> my food. It destroys all the vitamins.

5. Don't fly on that airline. It often <u>overbooks</u> and you might not get on the flight.

LANGUAGE UP CLOSE

Word formation often helps us to understand the meaning of new compound words because the new words are formed from two words we already know.

Example: One meaning of **over** in English is **more than.** "We received **over** 1,000 letters" means "We received **more than** 1,000 letters." If we say someone **overworks,** we mean that person works **more than** is necessary.

6 Listening in Context

Focus Strategy: Listening for context and specific details

Before you listen

A. PAIR WORK Discuss these questions.

1. Do you have talk shows on the radio or on television in your country?
2. If you do, what kind of things do people ask or discuss?
3. The doctor for today's talk show is a psychiatrist, what kind of verbs, nouns, adjectives, and expressions do you expect to hear?

Welcome to "Call the Doctor!"

First listening

B. Complete the chart. Indicate in column 2 the gender of each participant: *M* (male), *F* (female). In column 3, write where they are calling from. In column 4, check (✔) the speakers who get advice, and put a cross (✘) at those who don't.

Participants	Gender	Calling from	Gets advice/ Doesn't get advice
Psychiatrist			✘
Caller 1			
Caller 2			
Caller 3			

Second listening

C. Listen again and complete these notes.

	Profession	Specific Problem/Comment	Advice Given/Response
Caller 1	_____	_____	_____
Caller 2	_____	_____	_____
Caller 3	_____	_____	_____

D. PAIR WORK Compare your answers in C with your partner's and use his or her notes to add more information to your notes. Then discuss with the class the aspects of the talk show that interested you most.

Example: *It was interesting to hear that overexercising can be bad for you.*

7 Reading

Focus Strategy: Reading for specific information

Before you read

A. Answer these questions with the whole class.

1. Do you like to look at the moon?
2. What color does the moon appear to be in your country? Does the color change from region to region or season to season?
3. Are there any superstitions in your country about the full moon?
4. In your language, are there any idioms about the moon?

While you read

B. Read these statements. Then read the text and decide if the statements are *True (T)*, *False (F)*, or *Not Mentioned (NM)*.

_____ 1. The text mentions only the negative aspects of the effects of the full moon.
_____ 2. There are examples of some of the negative effects of the full moon in the text.
_____ 3. The text is based entirely on the superstitions of ordinary people about the moon.
_____ 4. In the Middle East, people tell fascinating stories about the moon.
_____ 5. Many scientists are interested in the moon and our moods.

READING UP CLOSE

Reading the questions before the text helps you focus on the specific information you are looking for. When you have found that information, go back and read the text again for pleasure.

CULTURE UP CLOSE

When people talk about a blue moon, they usually don't mean that the moon actually looks blue. A blue moon is when there are two full moons in one month. This doesn't happen very often, but it does happen. So, when people say, "Once in a blue moon . . . ," they really mean *hardly ever*.

Our Moods and the Moon

Does the moon affect our moods? For centuries, people in places all over the world have believed that the moon can affect us physically and emotionally. Now many scientists are also beginning to believe that this may, in fact, be true.

In particular, doctors suggest that the moon may have a negative effect on people who are already under stress. In some cases, these people can completely lose control. For example, New York's infamous murderer Son of Sam, whose real name was David Berkowitz, killed eight times, and on five of these occasions there was a full moon.

Staff members at psychiatric hospitals have long maintained that, when there is a full moon, patients become tense and uptight, especially at night. The influence of the full moon may also lead to depression. In a five-year study at Edinburgh's Regional Poisoning Treatment Centre in Scotland, scientists have discovered that many more suicides occur when there is a full moon. In addition, in his book *The Lunar Effect*, American Dr. Arnold Lieber, maintains that police and fire departments have commented that there may be a relationship between the full moon and an increase in violent crime.

On the positive side, some people benefit from the full moon. Fishermen know that this is a good time to go fishing because some fish are more active during the full moon. In particular, off the coast of Miami, this is a time when shrimp fishermen put out to sea.

If we accept as scientific fact that the gravitational power of the moon causes the tides of our great oceans, why don't we accept that it can affect our moods? After all, the human body is composed of 70 percent water.

After you read

C. Reread closely to find these facts.

1. The kind of people doctors say the moon may affect.
2. The reason why David Berkowitz became infamous.
3. The feelings of patients in psychiatric hospitals during the full moon.
4. The results of depression in some people during the full moon.
5. The beliefs of police and fire departments about the full moon.
6. The reason why some fishermen put to sea during a full moon.
7. One scientific fact about the moon.
8. One scientific fact about the human body.

 **Writing**

Focus Strategy: Sequencing events

W RITING UP CLOSE

When writing a particular type of document, it is helpful to have a model to work from. Try to make your writing style similar to the style of the document. This way the reader can easily identify its genre.

Before you write

A. GROUP WORK Julie is keeping a journal of her experience in the U.S. Complete her journal entry for today by answering the questions in each paragraph.

1. What did Julie do at work in the morning? What happened at the meeting?
2. Why did Greg get stressed out? What did he say to Mike? What did he say to Julie? What did Julie think?
3. How did Mike explain Greg's behavior? What else did Mike say about Greg's problems? What did Julie think about Greg's explanation?
4. What did Julie do on her way home from work? What did she hear about the moon and our moods?

> Wednesday, June 15th
>
> This morning I attended a meeting to check the arrangements for the e-commerce fair and my boss, Greg, got really stressed out because the flyers
>
> Mike says Greg is usually an easy-going guy but recently he
>
> On the way home from work, however, I tuned into this talk show on the radio and the psychiatrist answering the questions said that some scientific studies have shown that the moon
>
> Maybe Greg is not so crazy after all!

 Write

B. Write your journal entry for yesterday. Divide the entry into paragraphs according to time of day or memorable events. Remember to write about your feelings and emotions.

9 Putting It Together

A. PAIR WORK Choose an expression from the lists to describe your partner's condition or emotional state. Don't show the paper to your partner. Stick it to your partner's back. Take turns at guessing what is on the paper that your partner has put on your back. After you have guessed, take turns telling your partner a reason, imaginary or real, to explain this emotional state or condition.

Example: *You are tense.*

    A: *Am I relaxed?*   **B:** *No you're not.*
    A: *Am I stressed out?*   **B:** *Maybe, but that's not on the paper.*
    A: *Am I a workaholic?*   **B:** *No, you're not.*
    A: *Am I tense?*   **B:** *Yes, you are.*

    A: *Well, I am feeling tense because I am studying for a really important exam. I spend all my free time studying, and when I am not studying, I worry about the exam. I really hope I pass!*

to be uptight	to be easy going	to be relaxed
to be stressed out	to be tense	to be addicted to (coffee, tea, etc.)
to be burnt out	to be a workaholic	to be angry
to be depressed		

B. PAIR WORK Change partners and do the activity again.

Stay TUNED

STAY TUNED How long has Ken's grandmother been in the hospital?

A great age to be

Communication	Grammar	Vocabulary	Skills
Checking facts and observations	Tag questions for *be*	Age-related expressions	Listening to a talk
Requesting and giving information	Present perfect + time expressions	*Is anything wrong?*	Reading a newspaper
		Sorry to hear that.	Writing a profile
		Oh, no, that's too bad.	

1 Warm Up

A. **Look at the pictures and answer these questions.**

1. What do all of these people have in common?
2. What region of the world do you think each person comes from? Why?
3. Do you think these people still work or do you think they are retired? Why?

B. **PAIR WORK** **Discuss the following questions and report your ideas to the class.**

1. What is the life expectancy in your country?
2. Do men or women live longer in your country?
3. How important are grandparents in your society?
4. What roles do senior citizens play in your country?

2 Conversation

Bad news from home

Stacey and Casey arranged to meet in the park. They see Ken sitting on a bench looking rather sad, so they go over and try to cheer him up.

A. Listen and practice.

Stacey and Casey: Hi, Ken.

Ken: Hello, Stacey. Hi, Casey. How are you?

Stacey: We're fine, but you're looking a little down. Is anything wrong?

Ken: Well, I got some bad news last week.

Casey: Sorry to hear that, Ken. Can we help?

Ken: No, not really. My grandmother's seriously ill. She's in the hospital.

Stacey: Oh, no, that's too bad. You showed me some pictures of her once. You were very close, weren't you?

Ken: Yes, we were. She used to take care of me when I was a kid.

Casey: How long has she been in the hospital?

Ken: A month, and she's never been in a hospital before.

Casey: How old is she now, Ken?

Ken: About 92, I think.

Casey: Ninety-two! What a great age to be! You're lucky she's lived so long.

Ken: That's true, and she's always been so healthy.

Stacey: I hope she gets better soon.

Ken: Me, too.

B. PAIR WORK Discuss why Ken is sad. How do we know that Ken's grandmother has had a healthy life? What is Ken's relationship with his grandmother like?

ⒸULTURE UP CLOSE

By 2020 one billion people in the world will be over 60. So far, the oldest person for whom official records exist was Jeanne Calment of France. She died in 1997 at the age of 122.

GROUP WORK Would you like to live to be 100? Why or why not?

3 Grammar in Context

Checking facts and observations

Tag questions for *be*	
Positive statement	**Negative tag**
That's Ken over there, **We**'re on the right bus, **Julie and Mike** were in Colombia two years ago,	isn't **it**? aren't **we**? weren't **they**?
Negative statement	**Positive tag**
You aren't sure about the answer, **I** wasn't rude to him, **She** wasn't home yesterday,	are **you**? was **I**? was **she**?

The verb in the tag question is always in the same person and tense as the verb in the main part of the sentence. Use pronouns in the tag questions.

Answers can be a simple *yes* or *no* according to the situation. They can also be *yes* or *no* followed by more information.

Pronunciation

Use falling intonation on the tag question when you are sure something is right. Use rising intonation if you are not so sure.

1. That's Ken over there, isn't it?   (Sure)

2. We're on the right bus, aren't we?   (Not sure)

A. Write the numbers 1–8 on a piece of paper. If you hear falling intonation draw a falling arrow (⌢). If you hear rising intonation, draw a rising arrow (⌣).

B. Add a tag question to each statement. Use different intonations.

1. It's warm/cold out today.
2. You aren't a grandparent.
3. Ken was very sad this morning.
4. Overworking is bad for your health.
5. Your grandparents are still alive.
6. Our teacher wasn't absent last month.
7. We weren't at the game last week.
8. Casey and Stacey are healthy.

Interact

C. PAIR WORK Check your answers to A with your partner. Take turns asking for confirmation for each of the facts or observations. Think about which intonation pattern you should use. Where possible, give true information in the responses.

4 Grammar in Context

Requesting and giving information

Present perfect + time expressions	
Information questions	**Answers**
How long has your grandmother been in the hospital?	**For** a very long time. **Since** July 20th. **For** two months.
Questions	**Possible answers**
How long have you owned a car?	Not very long. **Since** 1999. I've never owned a car. **For** three years.

This use of the present perfect relates an action or situation that started in the past and continues into the present.
For tells us how long something has been true.
Since tells us the specific point in time when something started to be true.

Yes/no questions	**Answers**
Have they **been** in the hospital for a long time? **Has** your friend **finished** school?	Yes, they **have.** / No, they **haven't.** No, she **hasn't.** / Yes, she **has.**

Short answers use the pronoun and the auxiliary verb in the affirmative or negative form.

Practice

A. Complete the following text with *since, for, never,* and *always.*

Ken is very worried about his grandmother. She has been in the hospital **(1)** _____

a month and Ken's parents say she hates it because she has **(2)** _____ been in a

hospital before. Ken's grandmother has **(3)** _____ been very strong and healthy.

She's 92 years old and last year she was still riding her bike and working in her garden.

She has lived alone **(4)** _____ 1999, when her husband died, but she has

(5) _____ been lonely because she is very close to her family and friends.

Interact

B. GROUP WORK Use *How long* . . . and the cues in
column 1 to interview three classmates. Use notes to
complete the chart.

Action/Situation	Classmate 1	Classmate 2	Classmate 3
live in this town/city			
own a computer			
know your English teacher			
be a student of English			
have this book			

C. GROUP WORK Use your notes from the chart above to tell
the class about your classmates.

Example: *Ita has never owned a computer.*
          Ita and Miko have known their English teacher for a long time.

5 Vocabulary in Context

Talking about age

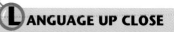

We use **baby** to refer to a child until he or she is about 18 months old. Another term for babies is **infants.**

We use **kids** or **children** to talk about girls and boys in general. When kids and adults do not understand each other's experiences, we talk about the generation gap. **Generation** is a group of people the same age.

We call **young people** between the ages of 13 and 19 kids, too, but we also call them **teenagers.** Another word for teenagers is **adolescents.**

People between the ages of 20 and 35 are **young adults,** and people between the ages of 36 and 65 are called **middle-aged.**

We usually call people over 65 **senior citizens.**

When a person reaches 100 years, we call him or her a **centenarian.**

Word formation

The meaning of a word we already know can help us understand new words.

Example: He had a very unhappy **childhood.** His parents died when he was 7.

Childhood refers to the state of being a child or the period when you are a child.

A. PAIR WORK Read the following sentences and decide if the bold-faced words have positive or negative meanings. Then, with your partner try to guess the meanings of the words.

1. "Don't be so **childish,** Pete. Remember you are 18, not 8."
   Meaning _____

2. "Ellen isn't 25, is she? Wow, I thought she was about 18. She seems so **immature.**"
   Meaning _____

3. "My grandfather's 68, but he's so **youthful.** He has so much energy, and he beats me at tennis!"
   Meaning _____

6 Listening in Context

Focus Strategy: Predicting

LISTENING UP CLOSE

Before you begin to listen, try to predict what you will hear in the listening from the context. This will activate cues to make your listening easier.

Before you listen

A. GROUP WORK Discuss the answer to this question: Do you expect grandchildren in the U.S. to have a good or a poor relationship with their grandparents? Why or why not?

disappoint = to not meet expectations

First listening

B. Read the statements. Listen and decide if they are T (True), F (False), or NM (Not Mentioned).

1. Grandparents in the U.S. today have an excellent relationship with their grandchildren. _____

2. Grandparents today help their grandchildren in different ways. _____

3. In the past, grandchildren in the U.S. had no time for their grandparents. _____

4. Today, parents in the U.S. are grateful for the help they receive from grandparents. _____

Second listening

C. Read through the notes below. Listen again and complete the notes.

1. _____% of American grandparents connect with their grandchildren:
   a. as companions.
   b. as _____.

2. Many grandchildren ask grandparents for advice about _____.

3. Parents in the U.S. today need help from grandparents especially with _____.

4. Grandchildren listen to their grandparents because _____.

5. There are _____ grandparents in the U.S. today and
   a. _____% of these are caregivers.
   b. 8% provide care on a regular basis.
   c. _____% are fully responsible for a grandchild.

6. Families that need help from grandparents most have problems with _____.

7 Reading

Focus Strategy: Identifying the main idea of a paragraph

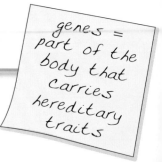

genes = part of the body that carries hereditary traits

Before you read

A. GROUP WORK Have you ever heard of the Okinawa Islands? If so, what do you know about them? If not, where do you think they are?

While you read

B. Read the topics in the list below. Then skim the newspaper article and choose the main idea of each paragraph.

a. influence of personal traits on the islanders' health

b. some of their typical daily activities

c. details of the islanders' diet

d. general information about their lifestyles

Want to live to be 100?

1. The people of Okinawa, Japan's *southernmost* region, live longer than anyone else in the world, and they spend a surprisingly large amount of that time healthy and active. We are not talking here about senior citizens suffering from dementia, who forget who they are and who cannot *recognize* their friends or family. We're talking about people in their 90s riding bicycles, digging up carrots, going fishing, and cooking their own food—in short, doing more or less what they did when they were 40! **Main idea:** _____

2. A recent study by a Japanese and two Canadian scientists has shown that the Okinawa Islands produce more centenarians *per capita* than anywhere else. What are the Okinawans doing right? The answer is they are leading very healthy lives. They seldom get stressed out over work. They express their emotions—love, anger, fear. They do not overeat, and they seldom *touch* fast foods. They are *surrounded by* loving family and friends, and they are into yoga and meditation. **Main idea:** _____

3. Some of the details in the study of these islanders are fascinating. For example, they eat a lot of soy, and, surprisingly, they *consume* a lot of *carbohydrate*s, so forget about Hollywood's high-protein diet and eat up your bread and pasta! Sweet potatoes and watermelons are also very popular with the Okinawans. **Main idea:** _____

4. Could it be that it is not diet and lifestyle which makes these people so healthy? Maybe it is their genes. But study has shown that when the Okinawans leave the islands and *adopt western lifestyles*, they quickly lose their health advantages, so it cannot be just a question of genetics. The study reports, however, that personality may also play a part. The Okinawans are incredibly relaxed and easygoing. They take things slowly and never *rush around.* **Main idea:** _____

After you read

C. PAIR WORK Write two *wh*-questions for each paragraph. Work with a classmate to ask and answer each others' questions.

Example: **Paragraph 1**

Q 1: *What kind of old age do the citizens of the Okinawa Islands have?*

A 1: *They have a healthy and active old age.*

Q 2: *How do many senior citizens on the Okinawa Islands spend their time?*

A 2: *They work in their gardens, go fishing, cook, and ride their bikes.*

D. PAIR WORK In pairs, try to guess the meanings of words or expressions in *italics* by (a) looking at the formation of the word; (b) finding a word in the text with a similar or opposite meaning; (c) finding an example in the text to illustrate the meaning; or (d) giving a simple explanation of the word. Share the meanings and explanations with the class.

Example: Paragraph 1 *southernmost* = south (n), so southern = adjective + *most*; *Japan's southernmost region* = the region which is farthest south in Japan

8 Writing

Focus Strategy: Organizing facts into paragraphs

WRITING UP CLOSE

When writing a text, it is important to organize all of the similar facts about one idea in one paragraph. Do the same with each paragraph. Then, organize the paragraphs into a logical order.

Before you write

A. Think of a senior citizen you admire. He or she can be a member of your family, a friend, a neighbor, a teacher, a famous person in your country, etc.

Write

B. Use the guide below to structure your profile.

A Senior Citizen I Admire

In paragraph 1, give personal data: name, age, gender, origins (town/city/country), daily activities, living arrangements (alone, with family, with a roommate).

In paragraph 2, give details of the senior citizen's: diet, lifestyle, health record.

In paragraph 3, give information about: the senior citizen's personality, your explanation of why he or she has lived so long, and why you admire him or her.

9 Putting It Together

A. Think of a famous senior citizen you are sure most people in your class know. He or she can be a writer, a politician, a TV or sports personality, a scientist, etc. Make a few notes about the person.

B. **PAIR WORK** Take turns guessing your partner's famous senior citizen. Follow these rules.

1. You are allowed to ask only 20 questions.
2. You may use only *yes/no* or tag questions.
3. At least 4 of your questions must be tag questions.
4. Don't guess who the person is until you have asked at least 12 questions.

Example: **A:** *Is this person a man?*   **B:** *No.*
A: *Is she a politician?*   **B:** *No, she isn't.*
A: *Is she a musician?*   **B:** *No, she isn't.*
A: *Is she an actor?*   **B:** *Yes, she is.*
A: *Is she from the U.S.?*   **B:** *No, she isn't.*
A: *Is she from Europe?*   **B:** *Yes, she is.*
A: *Has she ever won an Oscar?*   **B:** *Yes, she has.*
A: *She was married to a film producer, wasn't she?*   **B:** *Yes, she was.*
A: *She's Italian, isn't she?*   **B:** *Yes, she is.*
A: *She's still very beautiful, isn't she?*   **B:** *Yes, she is.*
A: *It's Sofia Loren, isn't it?*   **B:** *Yes, it is.*

Score: 15. 20 points for guessing the right person; penalty of 5 for guessing too soon.

Stay TUNED

STAY TUNED How long has Alan been living in England?

Exploring the arts

Communication	Grammar	Vocabulary	Skills
Emphasizing duration Talking about temporary actions and situations Commenting on actions and activities	Present perfect continuous Gerunds	The arts *It's something else.* *That isn't my cup of tea.* Word formation: nouns and adjectives from verbs	Listening to a TV interview Reading for biographical detail Writing a biography

1 Warm Up

A. Listen and circle the names of the famous artists and art galleries you hear.

Galleries	Artists	
Tate Modern	Picasso	Hokusai
Louvre	Warhol	Monet
Prado	Hopper	Rembrandt
Museum of Modern Art, New York		

B. PAIR WORK Work with a partner and list the names of art galleries, museums, temples, or other places of cultural interest in your country that might be of interest to visitors to your country.

2 Conversation

Junior year abroad

LANGUAGE UP CLOSE

In British English, *cheers* is sometimes used instead of *thank you, so long,* or *bye.*

Alan Jordan is in England, studying at a British university for one year. A local TV reporter is interviewing Alan about his experience.

A. Listen and practice.

Reporter: How long have you been studying at this university, Alan?

Alan: About 8 months now.

Reporter: Could you tell the viewers about the things you've enjoyed most about life in England?

Alan: All the culture. I love the old castles and cathedrals, and going to the art galleries and museums in London is something else.

Reporter: Which is your favorite gallery in London?

Alan: That's got to be the Tate Modern. The Picasso and Dali exhibits are very cool.

Reporter: And the disappointments, what haven't you liked?

Alan: Well, my big problem is that I haven't been concentrating enough on my school work.

Reporter: It is hard to focus when there's so much to see and do.

Alan: Yeah, that's it.

Reporter: Thanks for taking the time to talk to us, Alan.

Alan: You're welcome. Cheers, everybody!

B. PAIR WORK Discuss how long Alan has been in England. What are Alan's favorite things about being abroad? What doesn't he like?

CULTURE UP CLOSE

The Chicago Art Institute has been working with the Chicago public schools to broaden awareness of the cultural resources available in the school buildings and to integrate the arts into classroom curriculum. They have been doing this by introducing students and teachers to the recently restored murals in their school buildings. The study of these works of art encourage the preservation of the Chicago public schools' cultural treasures.

GROUP WORK Do young children take art classes in your schools? Are murals common forms of artistic expression in your country?

3 Grammar in Context

Emphasizing duration

Present perfect continuous

How long **have they been studying** here?
For about a year.

Why **have you been waiting** here?
Because the bus is late.

Why **has Alan been studying** Italian?
Because he likes Italian culture.

This use of the present perfect continuous is to talk about actions or situations that started in the past, continue in the present, and may or may not continue in the future.

The emphasis is on the **continuing or repeated** nature of the action. The action may also be **temporary.**

For permanent actions or situations, use the present perfect.

Contrast: Alan has been living in England for 8 months. (**temporary**)
Alan has lived in the U.S. most of his life. (The U.S. is his **permanent** home.)

Yes/no questions and answers

Have you been waiting a long time?
No, I **haven't.**

Has he been studying here for a long time?
Yes, **he has.**

Practice

A. Write sentences using the present perfect continuous.

Example: *Alan came to England in September. He's studying at a British university.*
Alan has been studying at a British university since September.

1. Alan started a modern art class several months ago. He is still taking the course.

2. Alan had his first visit to the Tate Modern last September. He still goes to the Tate Modern once a month.

3. Alan started to make English friends when he arrived in September. He's still making new English friends.

4. The reporter invited Alan for a cup of coffee at 7 o'clock. They're still talking in the café.

B. PAIR WORK Take turns asking and answering questions about the pictures.

Example: *How long have Alan and the interviewer been talking in the café?*
Since 7 o'clock. or *For two hours.*

1.

talk in café

2.

rain

3.

wait in line

4.

shop

5.

learn trumpet

 Pronunciation

C. Listen to the dialog. Write /ɪ/ when you hear a short vowel in *been* and /i/ when you hear a long one.

_____ **1.** How long have you been in England, Alan?

_____ **2.** I guess I've been here about 8 months now.

_____ **3.** And has it been a good experience or a bad one?

_____ **4.** It's been wonderful.

_____ **5.** Of course, I've been kind of lazy. I haven't done any work. All I've done is go to museums and art galleries.

D. PAIR WORK Take turns reading the dialog. Why do you think some people pronounce *been* as /bɪn/ and others as /bin/?

Grammar in Context

Commenting on actions and activities

Gerunds		
Going to art galleries	is	Alan's favorite pastime.
Making friends in England	has been	very difficult for Alan.
Playing the piano	helps	Alan forget his problems.
Overworking	has not been	one of Alan's problems!

The **–ing** form of the verb is called the **gerund** when it is used as a noun.

In these examples, the gerund is the subject of the sentence. When it is the subject of the sentence, the gerund can have its own object or it can be used alone.

Practice

A. Use the gerund form of the following verbs to complete the text.

make	join	read	live	learn	understand

challenge = something you want to do that is difficult and sometimes exciting

(1) _____ in a foreign country can be quite a challenge. To be begin with,

(2) _____ friends is often very difficult at first, and **(3)** _____

the customs of the new country is at times almost impossible. **(4)** _____ the

language, and **(5)** _____ about the history and culture of the country can

help with these problems, but they are not enough. **(6)** _____ clubs and

societies is a great way to meet people and to start to understand a new country.

Interact

B. Use gerunds with or without objects to complete these statements with true information about yourself.

1. _____*Watching*_____ TV is my favorite free-time activity when I am at home.

2. _____ is my favorite free-time activity when I am out.

3. _____ is the aspect of English that I find most difficult.

4. _____ is the aspect of my job/class that I like the most.

5. _____ is the aspect of my job/class I dislike most.

C. Interview as many classmates as you can until you find someone who enjoys some of the same activities as you. Tell the class what you found out.

Example: *Frank and I both like watching TV in our free time.*

5 Vocabulary in Context

LANGUAGE UP CLOSE

We use **an artist** for visual artists such as painters or sculptors. We also use it in a general sense for people who are very good at any of the arts. For example, Louis Armstrong was a great artist. He was a great jazz musician.

Talking about the arts

Look at the pictures, and read the texts. Discuss the meanings of boldface words with the whole class.

The theatre, music, literature, and dance are examples of **the arts.** Going to the theatre, museums, or concerts are examples of **cultural activities**.

There are different types of museums and art galleries, but the two main types are **traditional** and **modern.** In galleries of modern art, you can see the work of artists from this century and the last.

In museums, you can see **artifacts** such as **pottery,** furniture, clothes, jewelry, musical **instruments,** and, sometimes, **paintings.** For the most part, art galleries **exhibit** paintings and **sculptures.**

Folk dancing, folk music, and **local handicrafts** are examples of the **culture** typical of a country, region, or area.

Word formation

A. We can modify a noun or verb to form an adjective or noun. These new words are called *derivatives.* The new word can be an adjective (*adj*) or a noun (*n*).

Example: *to paint (v)*   *a painter (n)*
                                         a painting (n)
            culture (n)   *cultural (adj)*

B. GROUP WORK Look at these words. Write the original word and its derivative. Classify (*v, n, adj*) both the original and the derivative. What does each word mean?

New word	Classification	Derivative	Classification
dancer	*n*	*dance*	*n or v*
musical			
exhibition			
sculptor			
artistic			
dancing			
musician			
traditional			

6 Listening in Context

Focus strategy: Listening to understand globally

 **LISTENING UP CLOSE**

When listening, it is important to know the focus of your listening. You can focus either on the general idea or specific details. To listen globally means to understand the general idea of the text.

Before you listen

A. PAIR WORK Get ready to listen. Discuss these questions first with a partner and then with the whole class.

1. Do you like modern art or do you prefer more traditional forms of art?

2. Do you know the names of any famous painters or paintings?

school of art = group of artists with the same style of art

First listening

B. Listen to understand the context. Listen to the live TV interview and answer the questions.

1. Where is the interview taking place?

2. How many people does the reporter interview?

LANGUAGE UP CLOSE

That isn't my cup of tea means it isn't something I like doing very much.

Second listening

C. Listen for specific detail. Read the chart. Listen again and complete the chart.

Name	Origins	Occupation	Opinion, impressions, preferences
Jane			
Charles			
Nora			
Gemal			

Reading

Focus strategy: Skimming

READING UP CLOSE

A common way to read a magazine or news article is to skim it quickly for important details. It is not always necessary to read an article closely for all the information it contains.

Before you read

A. PAIR WORK Who was Pablo Picasso? Where was he born? Why did he become famous? What is his daughter's name? Why is she famous?

While you read

B. Skim the text and discuss the answers to these questions with a partner.

1. Which of the texts below is about Pablo Picasso's grandfather?
2. Which of the texts is a biography?
3. Which of the texts was taken from a book on art history?
4. Which of the texts is about a family history?

Cuban Picassos

Barbara Mejides, a Cuban historian, has a keen interest in people in Cuba whose last name is Picasso.

She has been studying these people for a long time and has made some amazing discoveries. Of the people she has interviewed, it seems that at least 30 are descendants of Francisco Picasso.

Francisco Picasso was Pablo Picasso's grandfather. He left Spain for Cuba in 1864 where he worked as a customs administrator in Havana. He also established a relationship with a woman named Cristina Serra. Francisco and Cristina had four children, and the 30 people Mejides interviewed are either the great-grandchildren or great-great-grandchildren of Francisco and Cristina.

There are musicians, carpenters, and doctors among these Cuban Picassos, but, so far Mejides has not discovered any artists. However, Gloria Molina Picasso is a fashion designer—just like Paloma, Pablo Picasso's daughter. Then, there is young Yoan Picasso. Yoan is an 11-year-old school boy and his passions are football and art, and guess how he signs his paintings? '*Picasso*' of course!

Pablo Picasso (1891–1973)

Born in Malaga, Spain, Picasso was without doubt one of the greatest artists of the twentieth century. With George Braque he established Cubism and then went on to introduce Surrealism. He lived in France, returning to Spain occasionally; however, after the Spanish Civil War he was reluctant to return to Spain at all. His most famous painting, *Guernica*, was inspired by war and was a reaction to the Nazi bombing of the Basque town of Guernica.

Among his many other famous paintings are *My Pretty* and *Night Fishing*.

After you read

C. **Read ONE of the texts again and answer only the questions for that text.**

Text 1
1. Who was Francisco Picasso?
2. Where did he go when he left Spain?
3. Where did he work?
4. Who was Cristina Serra?
5. Who are Gloria and Yoan Picasso?

Text 2
1. How old was Pablo Picasso when he died?
2. Which schools of painting did he establish?
3. Where did Picasso live most of the time?
4. Name some of his most famous paintings.
5. Where is Guernica?

D. **PAIR WORK** Find a partner who answered the questions to the other text. Take turns asking your partner the questions for the text you did not read in detail.

E. **PAIR WORK** Find words in the texts that are derivatives of the nouns and verbs in the box below. Classify the words (*n, v*, etc.) and discuss their meanings.

history (*n*)	discover (*v*)	administer (*v*)	design (*v*)	react (*v*)

8 Writing

Focus Strategy: Organizing events chronologically

Before you write

Ⓦ RITING UP CLOSE

One way to organize a written text is chronologically. This allows the reader to follow the text from one event to another.

A. **Use the information below to write a biography about Frida Kahlo, or use similar information about another famous person who has made a contribution to the arts in your country. Use the text about Picasso as a model to help to organize the biography.**

Name:	Frida Kahlo
Year of birth:	1907
Year of death:	1954
Origin:	Mexican
Profession:	artist
Other personal data:	• married to Diego Rivera • had a serious accident in 1925 • could not have children • no formal art training

Information about her work:	• influenced by Mexican folk art
	  subject matter = usually her own life, especially
	  her accident and its effects on her life

Famous paintings:	Viva la Vida, Las Dos Fridas

Write

B. **Use the same kind of information to write a biography about a famous person who has made a contribution to the arts in your country. The person can be a writer, a sculptor, a classical, jazz or folk musician/singer, etc.**

9 Putting It Together

A. **PAIR WORK** Imagine you are going to interview a visitor to your country/region/ city about his or her experiences as a visitor. List some of the cultural activities or challenges he or she might experience, and the likes and dislikes he or she might express.

Example:

Cultural Activities	Challenges	Likes	Dislikes
watching folk dancing	food = very spicy	people = very friendly	cities = very noisy

B. **PAIR WORK** Take turns interviewing each other, and use your notes in A to respond the questions. Start the interview by asking some personal questions.

Example: *Can you begin by telling us your name, and where you come from?*
And how long have you been living in _____?
What have you been doing here?

Stay TUNED

STAY TUNED What kind of car does Julie want to buy?

Make the world a better place.

Communication	Grammar	Vocabulary	Skills
Rejecting suggestions	*Too much, too many, not enough*	Transportation	Listening to a talk
Asking for confirmation of facts and opinions	Tag questions: *do/does* and *don't/doesn't*	The environment	Reading a leaflet on the environment
Making choices		*Forget it!*	Designing a poster
Discussing environmental issues		*I get the idea.*	
		That's about right.	
		Word formation: changing parts of speech	

1 Warm Up

A. **Label the pictures using the transportation vocabulary below.**

   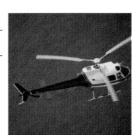

a. motorcycle	**c.** pick-up truck	**e.** boat	**g.** ocean liner
b. light aircraft	**d.** helicopter	**f.** minivan	**h.** SUV

 B. **Listen. Check in A the modes of transportation you hear.**

C. **PAIR WORK** **Interview your partner about the kinds of transportation he or she has used.**

Example: *Have you ever ridden a motorcycle? Did you like it? Why or why not?*

An SUV? Forget it!

Julie rented a car her first few months in the U.S. Now she is planning to buy one. Nick is helping her decide which car to buy.

A. Listen and practice.

B. PAIR WORK Discuss Julie's car preferences. Why doesn't she want to buy an SUV? How does Nick try to convince Julie that she should buy a sports car?

Nick: That SUV looks pretty reliable, doesn't it? Nice sturdy tires, anti-lock brakes . . .

Julie: An SUV! Forget it. They use too much gas, and that's bad for the environment.

Nick: Well, in that case, how about a small sports car. They're easy on gas. Look, there's one over there.

Julie: I'd prefer something safer. There are too many fatal accidents in cars like that.

Nick: If you drive slowly, you won't have an accident.

Julie: It's not quite like that, Nick. Anyhow, I'd like something bigger. There isn't enough room in a sports car.

Nick: Okay. I get the idea. You want a vehicle that is safe, big, and environmentally friendly.

Julie: Yeah, that's about right.

Nick: I know what you could do.

Julie: What?

Nick: Buy an electric train!

⌕ULTURE UP CLOSE

Seventy-five percent of all carbon dioxide emissions are caused by the industrialized world. The U.S. alone emits 25 percent of the world's total. This amount represents 600 million tons of carbon dioxide. A similar amount is produced by the entire developing world. The majority of these emissions come from cars, trucks, buses, and airplanes.

GROUP WORK Is anything being done in your country to reduce carbon dioxide emissions?

SUV (sports utility vehicle) = vehicle made for off-road driving, but popular for everyday use.

3 Grammar in Context

Discussing disadvantages and rejecting suggestions

Too much, too many, not enough + noun	
Count	**Noncount**
Excessive: too many people	too much gas
Insufficient: not enough buses	not enough room
too few buses	too little room

Too many + count nouns = **too much** + noncount nouns
Not enough + noncount nouns = **too few** + count nouns
Not enough + count nouns = **too little** + noncount nouns

Practice

A. Complete the text with *too much, too many, not enough, too few,* or *too little*.

Recent reports on the environment say that there is **(1)** _____ carbon dioxide in the air. For this reason, Julie does not want to buy an SUV. She says SUVs

use **(2)** _____ gas and cause **(3)** _____ damage to the earth's atmosphere. Julie is an environmentally conscious driver. Unfortunately, there

are **(4)** _____ people like this in the world today

so there is still **(5)** _____ carbon dioxide

emission. Julie would really prefer to bike to work because

there are **(6)** _____ buses on the route
between her apartment and her office.

Interact

B. PAIR WORK   **Use the cues to take turns making and rejecting suggestions.**

Examples: **1. A:** drive/mall   **B:** bike   **A:** (−) time
            2. A: eat at home   **B:** go/restaurant   **B:** (+) money

Conversation 1
A: *I'm going to drive to the mall.*
B: *Why don't you ride your bike instead?*
A: *I can't. I haven't got enough time.*

Conversation 2
A: *Let's eat at home tonight.*
B: *I'd rather go to a restaurant.*
A: *Going to restaurants costs too much money.*

1. **A:** drive to work/every day   **B:** take the bus   **A:** (−) buses
2. **A:** beach/today   **B:** pool/instead   **A:** (+) people
3. **A:** buy/new car   **B:** buy/ SUV   **A:** (−) money
4. **A:** fly/New York   **B:** travel/train   **A:** (−) time
5. **A:** live/Paris   **B:** prefer/London   **A:** (+) traffic
6. **A:** go/home   **B:** come/party   **A:** (+) work
7. **A:** order/pizza   **B:** cook/meal   **A:** (−) food/fridge
8. **A:** live/country   **B:** live/city   **A:** (+) pollution

4 Grammar in Context

Asking for confirmation of facts and opinions

> **L**ANGUAGE UP CLOSE
>
> Don't forget to use falling intonation on tag questions if you are sure of what you are confirming and rising intonation if you are not so sure.

Tag questions with *do/does* and *don't/doesn't*

Positive statement	Negative tag	Answers
That SUV **looks** pretty reliable,	**doesn't it**?	Yes, it **does.** I'm not so sure.
He/She **drives** a small car,	**doesn't** he/she?	Yes, he/she **does.** Yes, it's just a two-door.
The Jordans **own** a pickup,	**don't** they?	Yes, they **do.** Yeah, I think so.
They **try** to be environmentally conscious drivers,	**don't** they?	Yes, they **do.** Yeah, but it isn't easy.

Negative statement	Positive tag	Possible answers
Julie **doesn't own** a car,	**does** she?	No, she **doesn't.** Not as far as I know.
Sports cars **don't have** a lot of room,	**do** they?	No, they **don't.** No, they're very small.
We **don't have** plans tonight,	**do** we?	No, we **don't.** Yes, we're going to dinner.
He **doesn't** drive a small car,	**does** he?	No, he **doesn't.** No, he drives a truck.

Pronunciation

A. Write the numbers 1–7 on a piece of paper. Listen to the questions from the boxes above and use arrows to indicate if the intonation on the tag is falling (⌢) or rising (⌣).

Practice

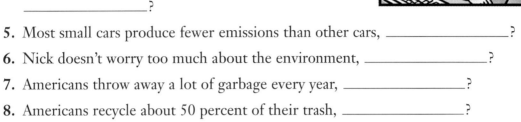

B. Add a tag question to each statement.

1. Julie has a car at home in Korea, _____?

2. She doesn't want to buy an SUV, _____?

3. She doesn't want to buy a sports car either, _____?

4. Some sports cars have very powerful engines, _____?

5. Most small cars produce fewer emissions than other cars, _____?

6. Nick doesn't worry too much about the environment, _____?

7. Americans throw away a lot of garbage every year, _____?

8. Americans recycle about 50 percent of their trash, _____?

9. All over the world, people dump a lot of garbage in the oceans, _____?

10. We need to reduce the carbon dioxide emissions in our air, _____?

 ## Interact

C. PAIR WORK Compare your answers with your partner's.
Discuss which facts you are sure of and which you are
unsure of. Draw the appropriate intonation arrow on the
tags. Then take turns asking for confirmation and responding.

Example: **A:** *Julie has a car at home in Korea, doesn't she?*
B: *I really can't say. Maybe, she does.*

5 Vocabulary in Context

LANGUAGE UP CLOSE

Pollutants are the elements such as benzene that pollute our air. *Pollution* is the effect of the pollutants.

Talking about transportation

Read the texts and look at the pictures. Then brainstorm the meanings of the bold words with your teacher and classmates.

Trains, buses, and **subways** are examples of **public transportation.** Cars, motorcycles, and light aircraft are examples of **private transportation.**

The buses, cars, motorcycles, and trucks on our streets are **the traffic.** When the streets are full of traffic, there is **traffic congestion.** When the traffic stops because of congestion, there is **a traffic jam.**

Cars, minivans, buses, and trucks are **vehicles.** An accident or **a wreck** occurs when two or more vehicles **collide.**

When choosing a car, you should first check the **tires, brakes,** and **engine.** If you plan to travel a lot, check the the size of the **trunk,** too.

Cars and other vehicles use **fuel** such as **gasoline** and **oil.** The **fumes** from these fuels **pollute** our air.

Practice

A. PAIR WORK Complete the text with one of the words or expressions in bold above or a derivative of one of those words.

Air **(1)** _____ is one of the most serious problems in big cities today. The polluted air comes mostly from the **(2)**_____ on our streets and highways. Air pollution is at its most dangerous in **(3)** _____ . The **(4)** _____ from the engines stay in or close to the **(5)** _____ because they are not moving. Therefore, drivers stuck in traffic jams breathe in very bad air. There are many ways in which we could help solve our problem with air pollution. We could use **(6)** _____ more, and private transportation less. We could also buy 'greener' cars, that is, cars with smaller or more efficient **(7)** _____ which do not use so much fuel.

B. PAIR WORK Classify (*n*, *v*, *adj*) the boldfaced words in the following sentences and discuss their meanings.

1. Many **environmental** (_____) scientists are convinced that our planet is getting warmer. The effect of global warming on the **environment** (_____) is very serious, as it causes extreme changes in our weather.

2. In some parts of the **globe** (_____), there have been more hurricanes because of **global** (_____) warming. In other parts, there has been no rain for months on end.

3. Every year, 29 million new cars appear on the planet. Car **manufacturers** (_____) should produce fewer cars and should try to **manufacture** (_____) vehicles with more efficient engines.

6 Listening in Context

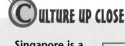

Focus Strategy: Taking notes

Before you listen

A. GROUP WORK Discuss the answers to these questions: What do you know about Karachi, Bangkok, Singapore, Jakarta, and New Delhi? Which of these places would you like to visit? Why?

CULTURE UP CLOSE

Singapore is a small island. The capital city is also called Singapore.

First listening

B. Listen and check the topics discussed in the text.

_____ Traffic problems in some big Asian cities

_____ The health problems of motorists in big Asian cities

_____ The cost of owning a car in Singapore

_____ The public transportation system in Singapore

_____ The origins of the people of Singapore

oxygen mask = facial covering that protects the wearer from toxic fumes

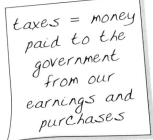

taxes = money paid to the government from our earnings and purchases

Word formation

C. PAIR WORK Adding endings to certain words changes them to different parts of speech.

Verb	Adjective	Noun	Noun
pollute	*polluted*	*pollution*	*pollutant*

Second listening

D. Complete the notes.

Traffic problems in Asian cities

1. One problem common to most cities: _____

2. Karachi's specific problem: _____

3. Jakarta's specific problem: _____

4. New Delhi's specific problem: _____*oxygen masks necessary on bad-air days*_____

5. Cost of car, and _____ taxes

6. Cost of special permit to drive the car: _____

7. Other costs **(a)** _____

   (b) _____

Singapore's public transport system

1. Types of transportation: _____

2. Cost of fares: _____

3. Capacity of city railway: _____

4. Alternatives to public transportation and cars: _____

E. GROUP WORK Compare the traffic in large cities in your country with the traffic in the cities mentioned.

7 Reading

READING UP CLOSE

Giving a personal opinion about the topics in a reading allows the reader to personalize the information in the text. This helps the reader to better understand the text.

Focus Strategy: Identifying the main idea

Before you read

A. Discuss the following questions with your teacher and the whole class.

1. In general, do people in your country care about the environment?

2. What do people in your country do to try and help the environment?

3. What do people in your country do that you think is bad for the environment?

While you read

B. Match the headings with the three paragraphs of the leaflet.

a. Help the environment when you shop   **b.** Help the environment when you drive

c. Help the environment when you travel

Doing Your Bit for the Environment

1. _____ In most countries, there are too many privately owned vehicles on the roads, so rent a bike and see the country that way. It is good for the country, and it is also good for your health. Catch trains and buses whenever you can. In many countries, public transport is cheap, clean, and pleasant. Save water. Use the towels in your hotel for at least two days. The citizens of many of your favorite vacation places may suffer because they don't have enough clean water.

2. _____ Buy products from recycled material. Try to find products with very little packaging. Re-use plastic or paper shopping bags. When buying electrical products, choose the most energy-efficient ones to reduce the electricity you use. Buy clothes made with natural fibers such as cotton, silk, and wool.

3. _____ Before you get into your car, ask the question '*Is my journey really necessary?*' The shortest car trips cause the worst pollution because the engine is cold. Share car trips with your family, neighbors, or friends. Check and maintain your car regularly. A poorly maintained car uses extra gas. Don't sit in your car with the engine going, as that wastes fuel. Don't keep unnecessary items in the trunk. If your car is heavy, it uses more fuel. Obey the speed limit. Driving at 50 mph can use 25 percent less fuel than driving at 70 mph.

After you read

C. PAIR WORK Decide if you should or shouldn't do the following things. Say why or why not.

1. ride a bike when on vacation
2. use buses and trains when on vacation
3. save water when you are on vacation
4. buy energy-efficient electrical products.

5. buy silk, cotton, and wool clothes
6. avoid short journeys by car
7. sit in your car with the engine going
8. keep heavy things in the trunk

 **Writing**

 **W**RITING UP CLOSE

Brainstorming or mapping out ideas for a creative project is a great way to begin. Write down as many ideas as you can on a piece of paper. Use your first ideas to help you think of new or related ideas. Then choose your best idea or ideas to create the strongest possible project.

Focus Strategy: Brainstorming and mapping

Before you write

A. GROUP WORK Work in groups of four. Choose a major environmental or energy problem in your country or city—for example, *traffic, electricity, water, noise, garbage*. Plan a poster to educate people about the problem. Think about who might see and read the poster. Where could you exhibit it?

Write

B. GROUP WORK Write the text for the poster, and prepare the artwork. Copy the text and artwork onto a large piece of paper.

C. GROUP WORK Exhibit your posters on the walls of your classroom, and read the other groups' posters. Discuss the posters with the whole class.

9 Putting It Together

A. PAIR WORK First, choose one of the situations below for your role play. Then, decide who is going to take the role of A and who is going to take the role of B. Next, work silently for a few minutes thinking of all the reasons for your position and the reasons against your partner's position. Finally, act out the role play, trying to convince each other that your choice is better.

Situation 1: A and B share an apartment. The apartment is a long way from downtown, where they both work. Public transportation has become very expensive, so they have decided they need their own transportation for getting to and from work. They don't have enough money to buy a vehicle each, so they are going to buy one together.

- **A** wants to buy a small car.
- **B** wants to buy a motorcycle.

Situation 2: A and B are on vacation together. They are staying on the coast, but they want to get to know other parts of the country.

- **A** wants to rent a car.
- **B** wants to rent bikes.

B. GROUP WORK Work with another pair of students and listen to their role plays. Comment on their performances.

Stay **TUNED**

STAY TUNED You didn't forget about the tickets, did you, Jason?

Let's forget about it!

Communication	Grammar	Vocabulary	Skills
Apologizing, and accepting apologies	Tag questions with *did*	Disagreements and apologies	Listening to a conversation
Asking for clarification	Possessive pronouns	*How could you. . . ?*	Reading a poem
Explaining mistakes		*It's just that . . .*	Writing a letter
Identifying possessions		*Right away.*	

1 Warm Up

A. Listen. The people in the dialogs are disagreeing with one another. Decide how strong each disagreement is—*not very strong, strong, very strong.*

Dialog 1: _____
_____

Dialog 2: _____
_____

Dialog 3: _____
_____

I'm right and you're wrong!

No, I'm right and you're wrong!

B. PAIR WORK Read the descriptions of the words. Listen to the dialogs in A again and decide if the people had *a misunderstanding, a quarrel,* or *an argument.*

C. GROUP WORK Discuss the following situations.

1. Have you ever had a misunderstanding like the one in A? How did you and the other person sort out the misunderstanding? Were you polite to one another, or did one of you get impatient?

2. What kinds of things might people in your family, work, or country argue about?

Quarrel: usually personal (between friends or family); it can be long or short

Misunderstanding: short, and not very serious; usually caused by confusion.

Argument: serious; can have a bad effect on personal or working relationships

2 Conversation

How could you forget?

Casey and Jason are having coffee in Café Puro. Casey asks Jason about the tickets for a concert they were planning to go to.

A. Listen and practice.

B. PAIR WORK Discuss why Casey was angry with Jason. Is this a short or a long quarrel?

Casey: Jason, you didn't forget about the tickets, did you?

Jason: The tickets?

Casey: Yes, the tickets for the Nana Mouskouri concert.

Jason: Oh, no! Casey, I completely forgot. I'm really sorry.

Casey: Jason! How could you forget? You know how much I wanted to see this concert! Plus, it's a UNICEF event, and I'm really interested in their work.

Jason: Casey, I didn't mean to forget, and I said I'm sorry. I'll call the ticket office right now to see if there are any tickets left.

Casey: Thanks, Jason. Look, I didn't mean to lose my temper like that. I'm so sorry. It's just that I love Nana Mouskouri, and I've never seen her in concert before. This was my chance to see her.

Jason: Don't worry about it, Casey. I'm sure we can still get tickets. Uh, Casey?

Casey: Yes?

Jason: I forgot to bring my cell phone. Could I possibly use yours?

⊙ULTURE UP CLOSE

UNICEF (United Nations International Children's Fund) was established in 1946 and won the Nobel Peace prize in 1965. The aims of UNICEF are to help children all over the world by financing and supporting programs to protect the lives of children and to improve their health, education, diet, and general development. Some famous people—especially actors—work for UNICEF on a voluntary basis. These people are called UNICEF goodwill ambassadors.

GROUP WORK Can you name any specific UNICEF projects or goodwill ambassadors?

3 Grammar in Context

Asking for clarification

Tag questions with *did*

Positive statement	Negative tag
You **got** a concert ticket,	**didn't** you, Casey?
Casey and Jason **had** a quarrel,	**didn't** they?
Jason **forgot** to buy the tickets,	**didn't** he?

Negative statement	Positive tag
Jason and Casey's quarrel **didn't last** long,	**did** it?
You **didn't go** for coffee with the others yesterday,	**did** you?
We **didn't know** about UNICEF before,	**did** we?

Don't forget:
- The verb in the tag question is always in the same tense and person as the verb in the main part of the sentence. Use pronouns in tag questions.
- Answers can be short positive or short negative according to the situation or simply *yes* or *no* with more information.

  You didn't go for coffee with the others yesterday, did you?
  No, I was in a hurry to get back to the office.

- When you are sure of the fact you are checking, intonation goes down (⌢) on the tag. When you are unsure, it goes up. (⌣).

Pronunciation

A. Listen and repeat.

Mike: You didn't forget to order the flowers, did you?
Jason: The flowers?
Mike: Yeah, the flowers for Casey and Stacy's birthday.
Jason: Oh, no! I completely forgot.

B. PAIR WORK Practice asking for clarification in the following dialogs.

1. **S1:** Are you going to the concert?
   S2: The concert?
   S1: Yeah, the Nana Mouskouri concert.
   S2: I've never heard of her.

2. **S1:** Do you like Julie?
   S2: Julie?
   S1: Yeah, the new woman at work.
   S2: Oh, yes. She's really nice.

3. **S1:** You bought the CD, didn't you?
   S2: The CD?
   S1: Yeah, the new Mouskouri CD.
   S2: Oh, yes, I did. Here it is.

4. **S1:** The Mexican chocolate at Len's party was pretty good, wasn't it?
   S2: The Mexican chocolate?
   S1: Yeah, he had a pitcher of it next to the other drinks.
   S2: Oh. I don't think I tried any.

L ANGUAGE UP CLOSE

When you don't understand why someone has said something to you, ask for clarification by repeating the most important part of what he or she has said. Use falling and then sharp rising intonation on the important part.

Practice

C. PAIR WORK Complete the statements. Add the tag questions. Decide if you are sure or unsure of the statement, and check the first or second column. If you have more information about the facts, add it to the More Information column.

Sure (⌢)	Unsure (⌣)	Facts	Tag	More information
		1. Alfred Nobel came from Sweden,	*didn't he?*	*Established a prize for peace.*
		2. Pablo Picasso didn't ever live in _____,		
		3. Frida Kahlo didn't have any _____,		
		4. _____ won the World Cup Soccer championship in 1998,		
		5. The Pilgrims arrived in the United States in _____,		
		6. Evita Peron came from _____,		
		7. Potatoes originally came from _____,		
		8. Jonas Salk invented _____,		
		9. The Americans didn't land on the moon until _____,		
		10. Sean Connery didn't act in the most recent _____ film,		

D. GROUP WORK Check all your facts. Remember to use the right intonation.

Example: *Alfred Nobel came from Sweden, didn't he?*
Yes, he did. He established prizes for peace, literature, medicine, and economics.

E. GROUP WORK Share new and interesting facts from *More information* with the rest of the class.

 Interact

F. PAIR WORK Brainstorm with your partner the things you might double check in the following situations.

1. You are going away on vacation and are on the way to the airport.

2. You have invited friends for dinner.

3. You are leaving tomorrow morning by car for a long drive to another city.

Example: **1.** *You locked all the doors, didn't you?*
2. *You didn't forget to buy the potatoes, did you?*
3. *You remembered to put the maps in the car, didn't you?*

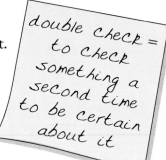

double check =
to check
something a
second time
to be certain
about it

4 Grammar in Context

Identifying possessions

Possessive pronouns

my				mine
your				yours
his	+	noun	can be replaced by	his
her				hers
our				ours
their				theirs

- Use possessive pronouns to avoid repetition of nouns.
  'This is my cell phone, isn't it?' **'No, it isn't yours. It's mine.'**

- Use possessive pronouns in answer to **'Whose . . . ?'** when you identify possessions.
  'Whose coat is this?' 'I think it's mine.'

Practice

A. PAIR WORK Complete the interactions with the correct possessive pronoun: *mine, hers, his, yours, ours, theirs.*

> Example: **A:** *I like your shoes.*
> **B:** *Thanks, I like yours, too.*

1. These are my CDs, aren't they?   Yes, they're _____ .
2. Did Jason forget his cell phone?   Yes, but Casey lent him _____ .
3. This is my English book, isn't it?   No, I'm sorry. It's _____ . It has my name.
4. Our house is small.   Well, you should see _____ . It's even smaller.
5. Do you have a laptop?   No, but my aunt and uncle lent me _____ .

Interact

B. PAIR WORK Take turns asking to borrow possessions from one another. Explain why you need to borrow them. Agree to lend some things. Refuse to lend other things. Suggest to your partner who might be able to lend them some of the things instead.

> Example: **A:** *Can I use your computer to send an e-mail? I'm having trouble connecting to the Internet.*
> **B:** *Of course, you can. I'm not using it right now.*
> OR
> *Sorry, I'm using mine, too. Why don't you ask Mike? He isn't using his.*

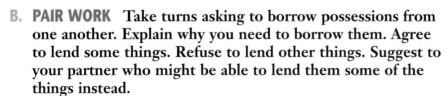

Talking about and settling disagreements

People usually **disagree with** one another because they believe they are **right** and the other person is **wrong** about something.

If you **lose your temper** when you disagree, then you **argue with** the other person. You can deal with an argument in two ways.

You can **apologize to** one another and **forgive and forget.** Or you can continue to be angry after the argument.

When people continue to be angry after an **argument,** their relationship changes. They don't speak to one another or do things together any longer.

When people in a romantic relationship have an argument, they sometimes **break up** and end the relationship.

When people forgive each other after an argument, this is called **reconciliation.** They both say they are sorry and become friends again.

Practice

A. **Complete the text with the correct form and tense of one of these words or expressions**: *lose (one's) temper, argue with, quarrel, forgive, apologize.*

Casey and Jason are usually a happy couple. They seldom **(1)**_____ each other but last week they **(2)** _____ over some concert tickets. Jason forgot to buy the tickets for a concert and Casey **(3)** _____. Fortunately, the quarrel didn't last long. They both **(4)** _____, and **(5)** _____ each other.

B. **PAIR WORK** **Discuss which of these expressions you would use in the following situations:** *Listen, why don't we forgive and forget; I'd like to apologize for losing my temper yesterday; sorry about that!; I'm so sorry. I've been very busy recently and...; oh, I'm sorry. Are you OK?*

1. You accidentally bump into someone in the street. You are both in a hurry.

2. You promised to call a friend you are very close to but you forgot.

3. You are in a line and accidentally step on the foot of the person behind you.

4. You have had an argument with a colleague at work. You don't want the argument to affect your working relationship.

C. **PAIR WORK** **Act out the situations. Use expressions like these in the responses:** *Don't worry about it; yeah, let's forget about it; that's okay; yeah, I think we were both wrong.*

 **6 Listening in Context**

Focus Strategy: **Distinguishing main ideas from**
specific information

Before you listen

A. GROUP WORK Discuss your favorite singers or music groups. Do
you know the names of any famous musicians whose songs are
about peace and reconciliation? Can you name any of their songs?

First listening

B. Listen for the main ideas and decide if these statements about
Nana Mouskouri are *T* (True), *F* (False), or *NM* (Not Mentioned).

1. Nana had a very easy childhood. _____

2. Nana sings only love songs. _____

3. Nana has other interests in addition to singing. _____

4. Nana has never had a tour in Germany. _____

5. Her next concert tour is in Asia. _____

Second listening

C. Listen again and provide the specific information for Nana's profile.

1. Personal information about Nana: _____ *lives in Switzerland* _____
   (origins, childhood, family, etc.) _____

2. Professional interests and activities: _____ *international singer* _____
   _____

3. Nana's character traits: _____ *hopeful* _____
   _____

4. Other interesting facts: _____
   _____

7 Reading

Focus Strategy: Interpreting poetry

READING UP CLOSE

When reading poetry the sound is sometimes as important as the meaning. Try reading the poem orally to "hear" what it says.

Before you read

A. PAIR WORK Discuss with your partner. Do you ever read poetry? What kind of poetry do you like to read? Can you name any famous poets from your country and from other countries? Who is your favorite poet?

While you read

B. Read the poem to get the main idea, and choose a suitable title from the list.

a. My Brother

b. A Sad Afternoon

c. The Quarrel

Discuss the reasons for your choice of title with the class. Then turn to page 59 to find out which is the real title of the poem.

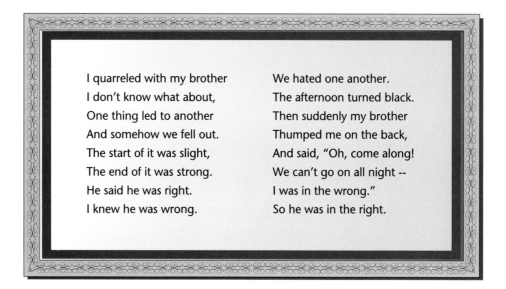

I quarreled with my brother
I don't know what about,
One thing led to another
And somehow we fell out.
The start of it was slight,
The end of it was strong.
He said he was right.
I knew he was wrong.

We hated one another.
The afternoon turned black.
Then suddenly my brother
Thumped me on the back,
And said, "Oh, come along!
We can't go on all night --
I was in the wrong."
So he was in the right.

one thing led to another = one disagreement created another one

slight = small, not very important

we can't go on all night = this quarrel shouldn't last indefinitely

After you read

C. PAIR WORK Read the poem again and answer the questions.

Facts about the poem

1. Do we know why the poet and his brother quarreled?
2. How do we know that it was quite a serious quarrel? Give at least two reasons.
3. When did the poet and his brother quarrel?
4. How did the poet and his brother feel about one another during the quarrel?
5. Who apologized first, the poet or his brother?

Interpretations of the poem

1. Why do you think the poet says 'the afternoon turned black'?
2. How do we know the poet accepted his brother's apology?
3. What do you think the poet is trying to tell us in this poem?

From page 58: Poem title: "The Quarrel"

8 Writing

Focus Strategy: Formulating a letter

WRITING UP CLOSE

It is important to identify the main points you want to communicate before you begin to write a letter. The final text will then be easier for the reader to understand.

Before you write

A. GROUP WORK Brainstorm things we do that we should apologize for. For example, we get impatient, we get angry with a classmate or a colleague at work, we forget to thank someone for a gift, or at home, we leave the kitchen messy.

Write

B. PAIR WORK Choose one of the problems in A and write a short letter of apology. Include the points shown on the notepaper.

1. Apologize and say what it was you did wrong.
2. Explain your behavior.
3. Express your appreciation of the other person's friendship or love and the hope that he or she will accept your apology.

C. PAIR WORK Find a new partner who wrote about a different problem in B. Read your new partner's note and reply, accepting the apology. Use this structure:

1. Thank your partner for the note.
2. Accept the apology.
3. Explain that you understand because you sometimes do the same thing.
4. Offer to forget about the whole thing and say you hope to meet again soon.

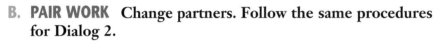

9 Putting It Together

A. PAIR WORK Work with a partner to role play the dialog.

Dialog 1

You are both finding your seats in an airplane.

A: Tell B politely that he or she has just taken your seat.

B: Show your ticket and insist politely that the seat is yours.

A: Examine the tickets and explain why you are sure it is your seat.

B: You realize A is right and you are wrong. Apologize politely.

A: Accept B's apology.

B. PAIR WORK Change partners. Follow the same procedures for Dialog 2.

Dialog 2

You have both just come home from work.

A: Ask B if he or she booked the tickets.

B: Indicate that you have no idea what A is talking about.

A: Remind B about the tickets for a trip the next weekend.

B: Confess that you completely forgot, and apologize.

A: Indicate impatiently that you are really unhappy about this, and explain why this vacation was important.

B: Indicate firmly that you didn't deliberately forget to book the tickets, and apologize again.

A: Apologize for being impatient and explain why you acted like this.

B: Accept A's apology and offer to call the travel agency first thing tomorrow morning.

A: Thank B.

Stay **TUNED**

 STAY TUNED Would you pay for an extra stop in Asia if you were Alan?

World traveler

Communication	Grammar	Vocabulary	Skills
Giving advice	The imaginary conditional	Travel talk	Listening to a dialog in a travel agency
Talking about imaginary situations	Gerunds	*I can't make up my mind.*	Reading a travel guide
Talking about feelings and interests		*Be on a tight budget*	Writing a journal entry
		Go for it!	

1 Warm Up

A. PAIR WORK How many of the numbered places on the map can you identify?

B. Listen and circle the names of the places you hear.

Mexico City	Bangkok	Singapore
Manila	Caracas	Seoul
Rio de Janeiro	Tokyo	Kuala Lumpur

C. GROUP WORK As a group, use the names in B to complete the map. Discuss the places shown on the map that you would like to visit.

2 Conversation

I can't make up my mind.

Alan Jordan has finished his year in England. He is planning his trip back to Los Angeles via Asia. His friends Toshio and Suchart are helping him.

A. Listen and practice.

Alan: Look! Student Travel has some great bargain tickets to L.A. via Asia.

Toshio: Which one are you going to take?

Alan: I can't make up my mind.

Suchart: Don't forget you promised to visit me in Thailand and Toshio in Japan.

Alan: I know. The problem is if I stop in Thailand, I can't stop in Japan.

Toshio: Couldn't you pay extra and stop in both Thailand and Japan?

Alan: Yeah, I suppose so . . . but I'm on a tight budget.

Suchart: If I were you, I'd pay the extra money.

Toshio: Yeah, so would I. How often do you get a chance like this?

Alan: I guess you're right. And if I made an extra stop in Thailand, I could take a train to Kuala Lumpur and Singapore, too.

Suchart: Yeah, and the train journey from Bangkok to Kuala Lumpur is fabulous.

Alan: And by the time I reach Thailand, I'll be fed up with flying.

Toshio: Go for it, Alan!

Alan: Right! I'm off to book my trip.

B. PAIR WORK Work with a partner to answer the questions.

1. Where is Toshio from?
2. Where is Suchart from?
3. Why at first is Alan reluctant to stop in Thailand and Japan?
4. Why does he change his mind?

© ULTURE UP CLOSE

In most university campuses in Europe there is a student travel agency, usually referred to simply as *Student Travel*. University students, teachers, and other people who work on the university campus can make all kinds of travel arrangements at Student Travel. They can buy train, bus, airline, and boat tickets for both national and international trips, and most importantly, they can get really good bargains—better than the bargains in off-campus travel agencies and even better than travel bargains on the Internet.

GROUP WORK Is there any similar place in universities in your country? If not, would you like there to be?

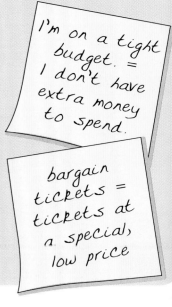

I'm on a tight budget. = I don't have extra money to spend.

bargain tickets = tickets at a special, low price

3 Grammar in Context

Talking about imaginary situations

The imaginary conditional	
If clause with *be*	**Main/result clause**
If I **were** you, **If** we **were**n't on such a tight budget, **If** Toshio and Suchart **were**n't his friends, **If** you **were** older,	I**'d** pay the extra money. we **could** take a trip to Asia. Alan **would**n't visit Japan or Thailand. you **might** not want to travel so much.
Use **were** with all persons of **be** including: **I, he, she,** and **it.** Separate **if** and main clause with a comma.	Main clause = **would, could, might** + verb, including **be** Use **'d** for **would** with pronouns in spoken language and full form in written language.
If clause with other verbs	**Main/result clause**
If Alan paid extra money, **If** they had the time, **If** we went by train and not by air,	he **could** stop in Thailand. Alan's parents **would** join him on his trip. we**'d** see a lot more of the country.
Use the simple past positive or negative form of regular and irregular verbs.	Main clause = **would, could, might** + verb, including **be**

Practice

A. PAIR WORK Take turns and match the *if* clauses on the left with the main clauses on the right.

1. If Casey could,
2. If Julie lived near the office,
3. If Greg didn't have to work so hard,
4. If Alan had more money,
5. If Casey and Stacey had the time,

    a. he wouldn't be so stressed out.
    b. they'd invite Ken to dinner.
    c. he'd travel to more countries.
    d. she'd work for UNICEF.
    e. she'd walk to work.

B. GROUP WORK Complete these imaginary conditions with the correct form of the verb in parentheses.

1. If I _____ more time, I'd travel by train and not by plane. (have)

2. If somebody gave us $1,500, we _____ it on a trip to Asia. (spend)

3. If the weather _____ warmer there, we'd visit England more often. (be)

4. If Singapore didn't have high import taxes on cars, the city _____ so polluted. (be)

C. PAIR WORK Take turns asking and answering questions about these imaginary conditions. Give reasons for your choice.

Example:

If you had more free time, what would you do?

I would take a dance class.

Oh really? Why dance

I've always loved dancing. When I was a kid, I used to be good at ballet.

1. You could choose which country to live in permanently.
2. You had more free time.
3. You lost your passport while you were abroad.
4. Your car wouldn't start in the morning.
5. Your best friend didn't speak to you at a party.
6. You spoke two foreign languages fluently.
7. You didn't like your job.
8. Your boss asked you to work late and you had tickets for a concert.

D. GROUP WORK Share with the class any interesting facts you learned about your partner.

Example: *If Kazusa had more time, she'd learn to play the guitar.*

Interact

E. GROUP WORK In groups of four, choose one of these imaginary situations and take turns asking for, giving, and listening to the advice of the other group members.

Example: You love your family. You get a job offer in another country.

A: *I just got a job offer in a foreign country. I'd make good money, but I love my family and don't want to leave them. What would you do if you were me?*

B: *If I were you, I wouldn't take it. Family is more important than money.*

C: *If I were you, I'd take the job, save money, and come back after a year or so.*

1. You've just won a trip and can go either to New York or Los Angeles.
2. You've noticed that a new person in your office is looking very unhappy.
3. You can't sleep very well at night and feel exhausted during the day.
4. This weekend Nana Mouskouri is in your city. You have enough money to go either to her concert or to a show of typical folk dances from your country.

4 Grammar in Context

Talking about feelings and interests

Gerund as an object of prepositions	
Be + adjective or verb + preposition	**Gerund as object**
Alan will be **tired of**	**flying.**
He is **interested in**	**traveling** by train.
Alan's parents are **looking forward to**	**meeting** his friends in L.A.

Other adjectives + *be* + gerund		Other verbs + preposition + gerund	
Be fed up with . . .	**Be** excited about . . .	to learn about . . .	to believe in . . .
Be sure of . . .	**Be** afraid of . . .	to start by . . .	to dream of . . .
Be good at . . .		to think about . . .	

Practice

A. **Complete with the gerund form of one of these verbs.**

fly	book	invite	live	travel

Since coming to England, Alan has learned a lot from his friends about

(1) _____ in Asia. He's very excited about his trip. He's particularly looking

forward to **(2)** _____ on some of the famous railways in Asia. Alan loves trains.

He likes airplanes, too, but he gets tired of **(3)** _____ very quickly since he can't
see much from an airplane. He's getting ready for his tour now. He's going to start by

(4) _____ his tickets. Then, he's going to buy some presents for Suchart's and

Toshio's families to thank them for **(5)** _____ him to stay.

B. **PAIR WORK** **Read the dialogs, and complete them with one of these phrases and
the correct form of the verb in brackets:** *I'm thinking of . . . ; I'm looking forward to .
. . ; I'm pretty good at . . . ; I'd be interested in . . . ; I believe in . . . ; I'm fed up with . . .*

Example: Why don't you fly to Singapore from Bangkok?
Because I _____ (fly). It's so boring.
Because I'm fed up with flying. It's so boring.

1. A: How do you travel when you are on vacation in your own country?

    B: _____ (travel) by bus. It's better for the environment than driving a private car.

2. A: If you had enough money, what kind of overseas trip would you take?

    B: _____ (go) to Egypt. There is so much to see.

3. A: Wouldn't you have a lot of language problems?

    B: I don't think so. _____ (learn) languages. And I already know some Arabic.

5 Vocabulary in Context

World travel talk

Sometimes when you travel you need a **visa**—official permission to enter, pass through, or leave a country. Visas are **stamped into** your passport.

It's always a good idea to buy **travel insurance.** If you get sick or lose one of your possessions while traveling, the insurance company will pay your **medical expenses** or give you money.

Before you travel, you should also have the **vaccinations** or buy the **medicines** you need to protect you against **diseases.**

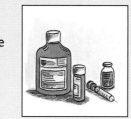

If you are taking a lot of **cash,** it's safer to carry it in a **money belt.** If you are taking a **credit card,** make sure that you can use it in the countries you are going to visit.

If you are on a **tight budget,** take a **travel guide.** Travel guides contain information about inexpensive hotels and restaurants. Don't forget all the other **essential travel items** such as a **camera,** a **hat, sunglasses, sunscreen,** a **pair of binoculars,** etc.

Practice

Complete the travel dialogs with one of the words from the texts above.

1. **A:** Guess what? I've lost my _____.

   B: Oh, no! Don't you have _____?

   A: Yes, I do, but that's not the point. The film in it had some wonderful pictures. I can't get those back from the insurance company, can I?

2. **A:** I'm going to Kenya on vacation.

   B: Aren't you afraid of getting horrible _____ like yellow fever and malaria?

   A: No, don't be silly. I can get a _____ against yellow fever, and I'll take some _____ to protect me against malaria.

3. **A:** How many countries are you going to visit when you go on vacation to Asia?

   B: Not very many. Some of the entry _____ are very expensive, and I don't have a lot of money. I'm on a _____.

4. **A:** Are you going to take _____ or a _____ when you go on vacation?

   B: I'm going to take both. My _____ says that it's a good idea to take a credit card for emergencies.

5. **A:** What three _____ do you always take when you go on a trip?
   B: Oh, I simply couldn't travel without my hat, my sunglasses, and a small radio.

6 Listening in Context

Focus Strategy: Listening for specific details

LISTENING UP CLOSE

Before listening, use the context to try to anticipate the kind of information that the text might contain. This will make your listening easier.

Before you listen

A. GROUP WORK Alan is in the Student Travel office, booking his tickets. Predict the kinds of questions he might ask the travel agent.

First listening

B. Listen to the conversation. Circle *T* if the statement is true, or *F* if it is false.

1. The travel agent helps Alan to save some money on his airline ticket.   T   F

2. Alan asks about train tickets as well as airline tickets.   T   F

3. Alan does not need to get any visas for his trip.   T   F

4. Alan asks the travel agent about the dates of flights from Los Angeles to London.   T   F

5. In general, Alan is very pleased with the service in the Student Travel office.   T   F

Second listening

C. Listen for these specific details.

1. Number of stops Alan can make on this tour: _____

2. Reason why the travel agent allows Alan to make an extra stop in Asia: _____

3. The train ticket the travel agent can book for Alan: _____

4. The train ticket the travel agent cannot book for Alan: _____

5. Advice the travel agent gives Alan about his money: _____

5. Two reasons why Alan is pleased with the service in Student Travel: _____

D. PAIR WORK Compare your answers with your partner's and discuss Alan's trip. Would you like to take the same trip? Why or why not? If you took it, would you make any changes to Alan's plans? Which changes would you make and why?

7 Reading

Focus Strategy: Skimming

R EADING UP CLOSE

When reading about places that are completely unknown to you, use your imagination to picture the scenes described in the text. Use your non-linguistic knowledge to help you understand the text.

Before you read

A. GROUP WORK What means of transportation do most people in your country use for long distances? Airplane, bus, train, or boat? What are the advantages of traveling by train on a long trip? Describe a train journey you have made or read about. Where does the train start? What is its destination? What cities does it stop in? What kinds of things can you see from the train on this journey?

While you read

B. Skim the text and match the main topics with the paragraphs.

1. Specific details: distance and schedule

2. The reasons why the E&O Express is one of the most luxurious trains in the world

3. Reasons why this is a wonderful journey

Sleeping or dining cars = sections of train where you can only sleep or eat

I. The Eastern and Oriental Express links Singapore, Kuala Lumpur, and Bangkok. This is one of the most luxurious trains in the world with air conditioning and private showers in every compartment. Traveling on the Eastern and Oriental Express is an unforgettable experience for other reasons, too. The Thai staff who work on board are among the friendliest in Asia, and the food in all three dining cars is absolutely delicious. (You'll need a special exercise program when you get home!) The scenery is varied: you will travel through rubber plantations and primitive jungles in Malaysia and beautiful farmlands in Thailand.

II. There are some very special attractions on this journey. At the end of the train there is an open observation car where you can stand and smell the jungle, listen to the birds, and breathe in the sweet Asian air. The evening entertainment is excellent and includes live piano music.

III. If you start your journey in Singapore, you will leave in the afternoon and the staff will serve afternoon tea immediately. One hour before midnight, the train reaches Kuala Lumpur, which has the most beautiful railway station in the world. The journey is 1,207 miles (1,943 km) and takes 42 hours altogether, so you will spend two nights and almost two days on the train and get into Bangkok after lunch on the second day.

After you read

C. PAIR WORK **Read the text again to find specific facts.**

1. Complete the information box with information from the text.
2. What kind of things can you see during this journey?
3. What kind of things can you do during this journey?

Countries:

Distance:

Length of journey:

Staff on board:

Special attractions:

 # 8 Writing

 Focus Strategy: Listing events chronologically

Write

 **WRITING UP CLOSE**

Comparing your writing to someone else's helps you to remember details that you may not have included. You can then include them in your work, using your own words.

A. Imagine you took a journey on the Eastern and Oriental Express. Use your imagination along with the information in the text to write a journal entry for the first 24 hours. Use this structure:

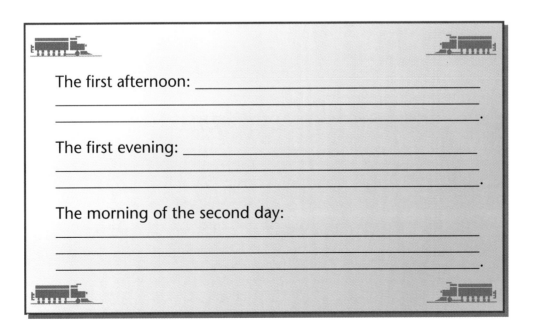

The first afternoon: _____
_____
_____.

The first evening: _____
_____
_____.

The morning of the second day:
_____
_____
_____.

B. PAIR WORK **Read your partner's journal entry and use it to add more information to yours.**

9 Putting It Together

A. You are preparing to study abroad for a year. You can take only one large suitcase and a carry-on bag. Make a list of what you would tand wouldn't take with you.

The things I would take and why	The things I wouldn't take and why

B. PAIR WORK Discuss your list with your partner. Take turns advising one another why to take or leave certain items.

Example: *If I were you, I wouldn't take an album of family photos. Take just a couple of photos of your family. An album would make you homesick. I'd take a pair of hiking boots. You might go hiking with friends . . .*

Reach an agreement about all the items, and complete a new list of items.

The three things I would take and why	The three things I wouldn't take and why

Stay TUNED

STAY TUNED How did Julie use to communicate with her parents?

Global messengers

UNIT 8

Communication	Grammar	Vocabulary	Skills
Talking about past habits, routines, and states	*Used to* + infinitive	Communication	Listening to a talk
Talking about recently completed events	Present perfect continuous	*No chance!*	Reading an article
Explaining present states		*Looks like it.*	Writing chat messages
		Don't even ask.	

1 Warm Up

A. PAIR WORK Label the means of communication.

_____

_____

_____

_____

_____

_____

 B. Listen to the dialogs and make a note of the arrangements the people make for future communication:

C. Which means of communication in A and B do you prefer when:

1. you are talking to your family and close friends: _____

2. you are on vacation: _____

3. you are shopping: _____

4. you need to contact someone from a long distance: _____

Give reasons for your preferences.

2 Conversation

Who won this time?

Nick and Julie are table tennis partners. They are just finishing their weekly game.

A. Listen and practice.

Nick: Oh, no, you win—again! Hey, have you been practicing without me?

Julie: No chance! I'm too busy at the office, but I used to practice every day in Korea.

Nick: Oh, look! It's been raining.

Julie: Yeah, it looks like it. Well, thanks for the game, Nick. I've got to go. My parents and I are going to 'chat' this evening.

Nick: That's okay. I've got to go, too.

Julie: I'm really glad my parents got e-mail. I used to call them every week, and it was so expensive.

Nick: Yeah, but if it's someone special, I prefer calling long distance. Voice contact is so important.

Julie: Wow! I didn't know you were a romantic. Look, here comes Mike.

Mike: Hi, there. So, go on, tell me. Who won this time?

Nick: Don't even ask!

B. PAIR WORK Discuss who usually wins when Nick and Julie play table tennis. How do we know this? Why does Julie have to go home right away? Which means of communication does Nick prefer when he is talking to someone special?

©ULTURE UP CLOSE

Table tennis is experiencing a comeback all over the world because, incredibly, it is better at getting you into shape than soccer or ice hockey, and it's even good for the brain. In Los Angeles and Japan, it is fast becoming 'the' thing to do after work. The game is the quickest racket sport in the world—and the biggest. It is played in 186 countries while tennis is played in only 138. Table tennis burns up about 245 calories per hour and is an excellent cardiovascular routine. Its effects on the brain are just as good: because you play one shot every two seconds on average, it trains you in thinking fast. It's like athletic chess.

GROUP WORK Is table tennis popular in your country? Are there formal competitions? Do you play?

3 Grammar in Context

Talking about past habits, routines, and states

LANGUAGE UP CLOSE

Because **used** is followed immediately by **to**, the **d** in **used** and the **t** in **to** become one sound: /t/.

Used to + infinitive

Positive statements

Julie	used to	practice	table tennis every day in Korea.
She	used to	call	her parents every week.
Casey and I	used to	play	tennis, but we don't play anymore.
Computers	used to	be	very big, slow, and expensive.

Negative statements

Julie's parents	didn't use	to be	on-line.
Nick	didn't use	to lose	at table tennis.
We	didn't use	to be	so fit and healthy.
Julie and Mike	didn't use	to have	to work so late.

Question forms

Did you	use	to enjoy	sports?
Did Nick	use	to play	table tennis with Mike?
Did Casey and Jason	use	to quarrel	a lot?

Use **used to** + infinitive to talk about habits, routines, states that happened regularly or were true some time ago in the past.

Used to + infinitive exists only in the past form. To talk about present habits, routines and states, use the simple present. Contrast **I didn't use to play table tennis** with **Now I play table tennis every day.**

The infinitive of **used to** is **use,** so questions and negatives are with **did/didn't** + **use** = **Did you/he/they/we use.**

Practice

A. Complete the text with words from the box.

used to	didn't use to	did you use to

Julie **(1)** _____ practice table tennis every day in Korea, but in the U.S. she plays only once a week. Her partner is Nick. Nick **(2)** _____ lose at table tennis. Then, he started to play with Julie, and he hasn't won a game against her yet. In Korea, Julie **(3)** _____ play for her university team, so she is very competitive. Nick learned to play table tennis at home with his brother and sister, so he **(4)** _____ take the game seriously. Now he wants to improve his game so he asks Julie for advice by asking her questions like these about her table tennis experience: 'How often **(5)** _____ practice?' **(6)** 'Who _____ play with?'

B. PAIR WORK First work alone. Complete the statements below. Reminisce about each situation.

reminisce =
to think,
talk, or write
about happy
memories

Example: *When I was a child, I used to go to beach with my family every summer.*

1. When I was a child,

2. When I was in elementary school,

3. When I was an adolescent,

4. When I started my first job, or my first year at college,

5. When I first started this English course,

Now, work with your partner and find out about his or her memories.

Example: What kinds of things did you use to do when you were a child?
Well, I used to help my Dad on our farm, and I used to . . .

Tell the class what you have learned about your classmate.

Example: *When Pedro was a child, he used to help his father on their farm.*

C. GROUP WORK Complete your section of the chart. Use your notes to tell the other group members about past habits or states that have changed for you with respect to each topic.

Example: *I didn't use to have a computer or send e-mails, but now I communicate a lot by e-mail.*

Topic	Student 1	Student 2	Student 3	You
Food				
Exercise/Health				
Communication	(-) e-mail			
Culture	(+) museums		(+) museums	
Environment				
Family				
(-) = things you didn't use to do		(+) = things you used to do		

D. GROUP WORK Take notes about what the other group members tell you and use the chart to share the information with the rest of the class.

Example: *Reiko and Rosa used to go to museums regularly, but they haven't been to a museum in ages.*

Grammar in Context

Talking about recently completed past actions

Present perfect continuous	
Question or comment	**Response**
What's the matter?	It**'s been** raining again!
Nick looks tired.	He**'s been** playing table tennis.
Hi, you're late.	I**'ve been** chatting with a friend in Italy.

This use of the present perfect is to talk about actions or situations which started in the past, continued over a period of time, and have just stopped. They are not happening at the moment of speaking but, often, we can see the results or evidence of the action/situation at the moment of speaking. *'Oh, no! It's been raining again.'* (It is not raining now, but the streets are wet.)

Practice

A. **Write statements about the pictures. Use the present perfect continuous tense.**

play	run	talk/phone	write letters
_____	_____	_____	_____
_____	_____	_____	_____

B. **PAIR WORK** **Use the cues on the right to give an explanation for the questions and comments on the left.**

Example: Nick
He was just talking to Julie.

1. There's paint on your shirt.   decorating/my living room
2. Why can't we go by car?   snow/roads/dangerous
3. Alan is in bed already.   travel/all day
4. The children are very hungry.   swim/all afternoon
5. Your eyes are red.   study late/all week

UNIT 8 *Global messengers*   **75**

5 Vocabulary in Context

Talking about ways of communicating

Although language is the most common form of communication, in most cultures **gestures** and **signs** are also used.

When people cannot hear or speak, they use **sign language** for **oral communication.** People who can speak and hear but cannot see, use **Braille** for **written communication.**

Probably the biggest **revolution** in the past 50 years has been in written communication in the form of the **fax, e-mail,** and **instant messaging (IM).**

E-mail, IM, and other **on-line** communications are not always suitable. People still need **regular postal services** and for the fast, safe **delivery** of important documents, they sometimes use a **courier** or **messenger service.**

In oral communication, the **cell phone** is also revolutionary. It has many advantages over **land line** telephones, but some researchers say that overusing a cell phone may be bad for our health. Also, cell phones are not as private as land line telephones.

Practice

A. **Complete the sentences with a word or expression from above.**

1. Could you please send the books by _____? I need them really quickly.

2. Be careful with _____ when you go abroad. A _____ in another culture may have a completely different meaning from a _____ in your culture.

3. Which do you prefer to do, call your friends or 'chat' _____?

4. At most international conferences, there are _____ interpreters to support people who cannot hear or speak.

5. Reading road _____ carefully is essential when you are driving, especially when you do not know your route very well.

B. **GROUP WORK** Use new words from the texts above to compare and contrast some of the ways in which we communicate today with the ways people communicated years ago.

Example: communicate with relatives in other countries
            We used to send letters to our relatives in other countries. Now, we usually phone, e-mail, or 'chat'.

1. send important documents
2. make emergency telephone calls
3. make all our travel arrangements
4. communicate with people who cannot speak or hear

C. PAIR WORK Take turns and match the sign with the interpretations/meanings.

Example: *This means that the water here is not safe to drink.*

a. You can't park here.
b. You can't turn left.
c. There are restaurant facilities here.
d. You can't smoke here.

e. You can buy gas here.
f. You can't drink here.
g. You may park here.
h. You may take pictures.

1. _____   2. _____   3. _____   4. _____

5. _____   6. _____   7. _____   8. _____

6 Listening in Context

Focus Strategy: Predicting

Before you listen

A. GROUP WORK What do you know about the origins of the way people live in your country? Which ancient civilizations have influenced your country?

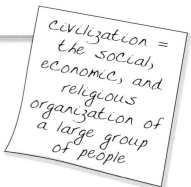

civilization = the social, economic, and religious organization of a large group of people

First listening

B. Listen and check the topics discussed.

_____ Different forms of communication used by the Incas

_____ Food the Inca messengers ate

_____ Size of the Inca empire

_____ The system used for the messenger service

_____ The names of some of the Inca emperors

_____ Two main functions of the Inca messengers

relay race = race where several runners cooperate to cover the distance

Second listening

C. PAIR WORK Listen again and discuss the answers to these questions.

1. Why was the messenger service important to the Inca emperor?
2. How far did the messengers use to run in one day?
3. Why did the messengers have to memorize the message?
4. What other function did the messengers have?
5. What is one difference between a modern-day courier and an Inca messenger?

 **Reading**

Focus Strategy: Skimming for the topic sentence

 **READING UP CLOSE**

Skimming is a technique used to find the gist of the reading. Read the possible topic sentences before skimming for the main idea. This way you can match the suggestions to texts.

Before you read

A. GROUP WORK Discuss: How many hours per day or per week do you use a computer? Do you think you use computers too much or not enough? Why? What do you think are some of the advantages of using IM?

 ## While you read

B. Skim the texts and choose the main topic for each paragraph.

1. Making new friends with IM facilities
2. Choosing your IM program
3. Considering the advantages and disadvantages of IM

I. With instant messaging (IM), you can use your computer keyboard to type a message and the person with whom you are communicating receives the message almost immediately. IM has the great advantage that it is fast and less expensive than making long-distance telephone calls, but it has the disadvantage that you can only exchange instant messages with people who are on-line at the same time as you. _____

II. There are several IM programs, but the best is the one your friends are using. If they are not using an IM, then choose the messenger where most of your friends have their email addresses. To install an IM, go to the program's home page and follow the step-by-step installation guide. You will find that common programs have two main parts: a message box and a control console. _____

III. Of course, instant messaging is no fun if you have no one to chat with. If you have no one to chat with, go back to the messaging console. By clicking on the Chat icon, you can join a chat room from the options provided. If you find a chat room you think you will enjoy, highlight it and click the button Go to Room. Even on your first visit to a chat room, you are sure to make at least one 'electronic' friend. _____

After you read

C. Read and find the specific information to answer these questions.

1. What are the advantages of using IM?
2. What is one disadvantage?
3. Which is the best IM program for you?
4. Where do you find the instructions for installing an IM?
5. What happens when you click on Chat?
6. How do you get into a chat room which you think you will like?
7. What is one advantage of joining a chat room?

 **8 Writing**

 **W**RITING UP CLOSE

When writing e-mails or chatting through IM, be sure to read your response before sending it, to get the feel of what you have said. Ask yourself if you would say the same thing in person.

Focus Strategy: Instant messaging

Before you write

A. PAIR WORK Work with a partner. Imagine that you are friends who live far from each other, but can use IM to communicate. Brainstorm the kinds of topics you might write to each other about.

 ## Write

B. Decide who is Student 1 and who is Student 2. Then pretend you are using IM. Write notes to each other following the messaging instructions:

Student 1: Write a short greeting to Student 2 to check that he or she is on line and ready to 'chat'. (*Pass your paper to Student 2.*)

Student 2: Read the message from Student 1 and write a short response. (*Pass the paper back to Student 1.*)

Student 1: Read Student 2's message and write a short question asking him or her for information about one of the topics you discussed in A. (*Pass the paper to Student 2 again.*)

Student 2: Read Student 1's message, and write a response. Then explain to Student 1 that you have to go to class and suggest a time when you can chat again. (*Pass the paper to Student 1 again.*)

Student 1: Read Student 2's message. Write a response thanking Student 2 for the information and agreeing to the time suggested for another chat. (*Pass the paper to Student 2 for the last time.*)

9 Putting It Together

A. First work alone and check the items in the list that are true about you.

	Me	Other Students
1. used to write a lot of letters but now prefer to send e-mails		
2. didn't use to like computers but use them a lot now		
3. used to send a lot of e-mails but now prefer face-to-face communication		
4. didn't use to own a cell phone but now have one for emergencies		
5. didn't use to chat but now chat often		
6. used to talk on the phone a lot but now prefer to 'chat'		
7. used to own a cell phone but lost it		
8. used to surf the Internet all the time but now prefer to go to a library		

B. GROUP WORK Now mingle with your classmates until you find a person for each of the habits or situations in A above. Write their names under *Other Students*.

Example:

You: Hi, Chris. Do you like to send e-mails?

Chris: Yes, I do.

You: Before you got e-mail, did you use to write a lot of letters?

Chris: No, I didn't. I have never written a lot of letters.

C. Share the information you have gathered with the whole class.

Example: *Chris and I both love to send e-mails. Before we got computers, I used to write a lot of letters but Chris has never written a lot of letters.*

Stay TUNED

STAY TUNED Do you think you would be able to do this kind of work?

Tough choices

Communication	Grammar	Vocabulary	Skills
Introducing a sensitive topic	*Could* to express alternatives	Emergencies and disasters	Listening to a talk
Expressing support	*Have to* and *be able to:* future form	*I've been thinking . . .*	Reading a poem
Expressing alternatives	Compound modifiers	*I'm with you all the way.*	Writing a personal letter
Using compact descriptions		*How would you feel if . . .*	
		Word formation: nouns + *-ous*	

1 Warm Up

A. What has caused the problems in pictures 1–3? Has your country ever had a similar problem, or do you know about any country that has suffered because of these problems? When people suffer because of emergencies like these, who helps them?

1.

2.

3.

B. Listen and take notes about the kind of volunteer work each person is going to do.

C. PAIR WORK If you could do volunteer work, what kind of work would you do? Why? Would you do it in your own country or abroad? Why?

> volunteer (n) = a person who offers his or her professional services free

> Volunteer (adj) = work that is offered and done for free

2 Conversation

Breaking the news

Jason and Casey are out for a walk.

A. Listen and practice.

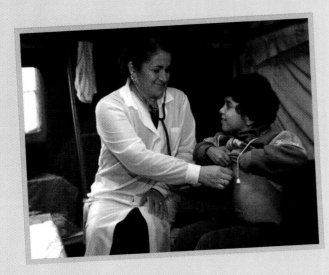

B. PAIR WORK Why does Casey break this news gently to Jason? What is Jason's main worry with respect to Casey's plan? How long would Casey be working in another country?

Casey: Jason, I've been thinking . . .

Jason: About what?

Casey: Well, how would you feel if I went to work in a foreign country after I finish medical school?

Jason: Well, I'd miss you a lot but if it's what you want, you should go.

Casey: I'd like to do volunteer work.

Jason: Oh yeah? With which organization?

Casey: I was thinking, I could work for UNICEF, or I could join MSF, or . . .

Jason: What does MSF stand for?

Casey: Medecins sans Frontiers. They work in refugee camps all over the world.

Jason: Hey, that sounds dangerous.

Casey: I know. I'll have to be careful, but it would only be a six-month contract.

Jason: Wow, Casey! This is a big decision. But I'm with you all the way.

Casey: Oh, Jason, thank you so much for supporting me. I knew you'd understand.

ⓒ ULTURE UP CLOSE

Medicins sans Frontiers (MSF), which is French for *Doctors Without Borders,* is an international organization. It works from five centers in Europe: France, Belgium, Switzerland, Spain, and Luxembourg. Each year it sends 200 volunteers, including doctors, nurses, and other healthcare workers, to an average of 70 countries. The volunteers work in camps with refugees who have had to leave their homes because of war, religious persecution, or a natural disaster. MSF operates on a rapid-response basis, guaranteeing to be at a camp within 24–36 hours. Money to support the work of MSF comes from voluntary donations from individuals and businesses around the world.

refugee = a person who has to leave his or her country or region because of an emergency

GROUP WORK What are the names of your local volunteer groups? What are their functions?

3 Grammar in Context

Expressing alternatives

Could, will/won't have to, might/not be able to

Could

Alternative 1: Casey **could** work for UNICEF and help with projects for children.
Alternative 2: She **could** work with MSF in an international refugee camp.
Alternative 3: She **could** stay in the U.S. and start her medical residency right away.

To list alternatives, use ***could*** + verb.

Will have to/won't have to, will/won't/might/might not be able to

She **will have to** be very careful if she goes to work in a refugee camp.
She **won't have to** study anymore.
She **won't be able to** do all the things she did in L.A.
She **might be able to** go on-line and 'chat' with Jason.
She **might not be able to** relax. The work is quite stressful.

Will have to/won't have to + verb and ***might/might not be able to*** + verb are useful when you are evaluating the alternatives.

Practice

Complete the dialog with one of these words or expressions.

could	will be able to	might not be able to	won't be able to

Jason: Casey's thinking of doing volunteer work overseas when she graduates.

Mike: She's crazy. She **(1)** _____ make any money with that kind of work.

Jason: Maybe not, but she **(2)** _____ put all the things she has learned into practice.

Mike: Yeah, but she **(3)** _____ do that here, too, or she **(4)** _____ do her residency immediately. But volunteer work overseas—forget it. She **(5)** _____ have any fun.

Jason: I'm not so sure about that. She **(6)** _____ have the kind of fun we have now, but I bet she'll get a lot of satisfaction out of her work.

Mike: Dream on, Jason. My guess is she'll come back to L.A. after the first month.

> Well, you could . . .

> Or I could . . .

4 Grammar in Context

Using compact descriptions

Compound modifiers

Adjective + noun = compound adjective

Casey had a **forty-minute** interview for her contract with MSF.

It's only a **six-month** contract.

MSF functions in many **high-risk** areas of the world.

It operates on a **rapid-response** basis.

Make your descriptions shorter and sharper by combining adjectives + nouns and using them as one adjective. *Casey had an interview with MSF. It lasted forty minutes. = Casey had a forty-minute interview.*

Omit the plural *s'* of nouns when they are used in compound adjectives.

Use a hyphen between the adjective and the noun to show that they are one adjective.

Some compound adjectives have three parts. *She has a daughter. Her daughter is six years old. = She has a six-year-old daughter.*

Noun + adjective = compound adjective

MSF is a **world-famous** organization.

It sometimes operates in some **French-speaking** countries.

It usually works with sick and **poverty-stricken** refugees.

Make your descriptions shorter and sharper by combining nouns + adjectives and using them as one adjective. *MSF is a famous organization. People all over the world know about it. = MSF is a world-famous organization.*

Use a hyphen between the noun and the adjective to show that they are one adjective.

Practice

A. **GROUP WORK** First work alone. Read the following sentences and decide what each one means. Then compare your ideas with the other members of the group.

Example: In some regions of the world there are man-eating crocodiles.
In some regions of the world there are crocodiles which eat people.

1. Many international emergency services use American-built helicopters.

2. During the last earthquake in Japan, many five-story buildings collapsed.

3. Some emergency workers have to fly into danger zones in single-engine airplanes.

4. Many international emergency projects are with camp-based refugees.

B. PAIR WORK Rewrite the following descriptions, making them shorter by using compound modifiers.

1. UNICEF has just appointed a new director. He was **educated** in the **U.S.**

2. Casey will have **a training program** before she goes abroad. It will last **three weeks.**

3. Casey has also decided to take **an optional course.** She wants to study the basics of a **foreign language** before she leaves.

4. Jason is worried about **Casey's work.** He says the **risks** involved are **high.**

5. Before Casey leaves they are going to take **a vacation.** They are going to rest and relax for **five days.**

5 Vocabulary in Context

Talking about disasters and emergencies

Floods, hurricanes, and **earthquakes** are some common types of **natural disasters.**

National **emergency services,** such as the **fire** and **ambulance services,** help people who are the **victims** of a disaster.

Famine, drought, and **forest fires** also cause emergencies and, like war and **persecution,** often force people to leave their homes, so many end up in **refugee camps.**

When there are **large-scale** disasters, international **aid organizations** usually send help in the form of food, clothes, medicines, and **medical personnel** such as volunteer doctors and nurses.

Practice

A. PAIR WORK Complete each sentence with one of the words from the texts above.

1. There's been another _____ in California, and the firefighters are working day and night.

2. We need to send more food aid to Ethiopia. Apparently, it hasn't been raining there for months so there's a _____.

3. Yeah, and there's a _____ in the Sudan. The farmers planted their crops but they didn't grow, so the people haven't had food for months.

4. Did you see the pictures of the _____ in Turkey on the TV? Weren't the emergency services brilliant? They rescued a kid from a building 5 days after it collapsed.

5. I don't think I could work in a _____. I'd find all the human suffering totally heart-breaking.

Word formation

B. You can form adjectives by adding *-ous* to some nouns. Complete the chart.

Noun	Adjective
danger	*dangerous*
mountain	
	poisonous
humor	
	disastrous
*mystery	
	famous**
*glory	
**nerve	

*Change the *y* to *i* in adjective form.
**Drop the *e* from the noun when forming the adjective.

C. Use adjectives from the chart to brainstorm true facts about your country or region.

Example: *Poisonous snakes are common in the southern region of our country.*

D. PAIR WORK You have to discuss a sensitive topic with someone. Match the introductory expressions in this list with the situations below. Role play a dialog for each situation with your partner.

> Could I have a quick word with you?
> I've been thinking . . .
> Could we possibly make a time to talk later on?
> How would you feel if . . . ?
> I was wondering if we could talk about . . .

1. You have to tell your parents you are going to do volunteer work in another country.

2. You have decided to break up with your partner.

3. You want to tell your boss that he or she is giving you too much work.

4. You have to tell your partner that you are planning to go abroad for a while.

5. You notice that one of your best restaurant employees is not wearing his or her uniform today.

6 Listening in Context

Focus Strategy: Predicting

Before you listen

A. PAIR WORK You are going to hear a volunteer doctor talk about his experience in a refugee camp. Check in column 1 the words and expression in the list that you predict he might use.

Before you listen	First listening	Words
		challenge
		dangers
		worried
		nervous
		victims
		poisonous
		humor
		hope

First listening

B. Listen and check the words in column 2 that he actually uses.

Second listening

C. PAIR WORK Listen again. First work alone and answer the questions. Then compare your answers with your partner's.

1. How long did the doctor work in the refugee camp?

2. What did he find difficult about living and working in the camp?

3. Why did the attitude of the refugees change after the second month?

4. Would this doctor make the same choice again? Why, or why not?

5. What advice does he give to people who are thinking about doing volunteer work abroad?

 # Reading

Focus Strategy: Interpreting meaning

Before you read

A. **GROUP WORK** What kind of poetry do you prefer? Poetry about nature, about love, about war? Can you name any poems that are famous in your language? Can you say a little about the poet?

 ## While you read

B. Read the poem silently as your teacher reads it aloud or as you listen to the tape. Then answer the questions.

1. Where is the poet?
2. What time of day is it?
3. What decision does he have to make?
4. Does he find it easy or difficult to make the decision?
5. Who wrote the poem?

diverge = separate

undergrowth = plants and bushes that grow below trees.

want wear = not used a lot

to tread (trod, trodden) = to walk on

sigh = deep, slow breath to indicate tiredness or sadness.

The Road Not Taken

Two roads diverged in a yellow wood,
And sorry I could not travel both
And be one traveler, long I stood
And looked down one as far as I could
To where it bent in the undergrowth.

Then took the other as just as fair,
And having perhaps the better claim,
Because it was grassy and wanted wear,
Though as for that the passing there
Had worn them really about the same,

And both that morning equally lay
In leaves no step had trodden back.
Oh, I kept the first for another day!
Yet knowing how way leads to way,
I doubted if I should ever come back.

I shall be telling this with a sigh

Somewhere ages and ages hence.
Two roads diverged in a wood and I—
I took the one less travelled by,
And that has made all the difference.

Robert Frost

About the poet: Robert Lee Frost (1874–1963) was born in California, but lived most of his life in New England. At first, Americans did not like his poetry about the reality of rural life because they preferred poetry with more complex images and thoughts. He spent some time in Great Britain, where he published his first two collections *A Boy's Will* and *North of Boston.* Things changed for Frost when he returned to the United States, where he became known and loved by many Americans. He died in Boston on January 29, 1963.

After you read

C. PAIR WORK Read the poem silently again. Then with your partner, find evidence for the following ideas:

1. The poet would like to travel along both roads.
2. The poet chooses the road most people don't take.
3. The poet does not think he will be able to come back and try the other road.
4. This was an important decision and he will never forget the day he took it.

D. GROUP WORK Discuss the answers to these questions.

1. What is the poet saying about life in this poem?
2. Who do you think the poet might tell about this decision? Why might he tell about it 'with a sigh'?
3. What does 'I took the one less travelled by and that has made all the difference' mean?

WRITING UP CLOSE

Using common expressions makes your writing sound more natural and appropriate. It is also important to use the correct level of formality when using these expressions.

8 Writing

Focus Strategy: Selecting appropriate expressions

Before you write

A. GROUP WORK In groups of four, discuss difficult decisions you have made in the past or a difficult decision you might have to make in the future.

Write

B. Write a short letter to someone close to you telling him or her of a difficult decision you have just made that might make this person worry. Use this structure:

1. Open the letter with a greeting and ask how the person is doing.
2. Remind the person about the decision you had to make.
3. Gently tell the person what you have decided.
4. Explain why you made the decision you made.
5. Ask the person not to worry.
6. End the letter on a positive note, promising to keep in touch.

9 Putting It Together

A. PAIR WORK First work alone. Read the situations below. Then with your partner decide which situation you are going to role play. Choose your roles. Take a few minutes to prepare them. Then act out the role plays.

1. Two roommates have shared an apartment for a long time and have had a very good relationship.

Are you busy? Can I have a word with you?

| **Role 1**
Roommate 1: you have just gotten a better job, and you want to buy your own apartment. You have to tell Roommate 2 gently about your decision to move out and thank him or her for the good times. | **Role 2**
Roommate 2: Roommate 1 tells you about his or her decision to move out. You are very sorry about this but congratulate him or her on his success and promise to keep in touch. |

2. A company director and his or her assistant director have worked together for a long time, have run a very successful business, and have had a good working relationship.

| **Role 1**
Assistant director: You are tired of the business world and have decided to give up your job and do volunteer work overseas with a small farming cooperative. Prepare to break the news gently to the company director, explain why you made your decision, and to defend it when the director expresses serious doubts about it. | **Role 2**
Company director: Your assistant director tells you that he or she is going to resign and go to a foreign country to do volunteer work. Prepare to tell him or her why you think this is a crazy decision and all the reasons why he or she might be sorry he or she made it. Accept the decision reluctantly and wish the assistant director all the best and promise to keep in touch. |

Stay TUNED

B. GROUP WORK Join a pair of students who did the other role play. Take turns listening as you act out your roles. Then change situations. Take time to prepare and act out the role plays.

STAY TUNED Did Alan hurt himself?

Take care of yourself!

Communication	Grammar	Vocabulary	Skills
Talking about new and established routines	*Be used to* + noun/gerund	Body parts; aches, pains, and injuries	Listening to dialogs about aches and pains
Talking about self-directed activities	*Get used to* + noun/gerund	*Watch this!*	Reading a magazine article
Talking about aches, pains, and injuries	Reflexive pronouns	*Don't be silly!*	Writing an outline
		I think I'll pass.	

1 Warm Up

A. Listen and circle the words you hear.

heels	shoulders	elbows	chest
knees	wrist	toes	thighs
neck	waist	ankles	hips

B. PAIR WORK Use the words from A and other words you know to label the body parts.

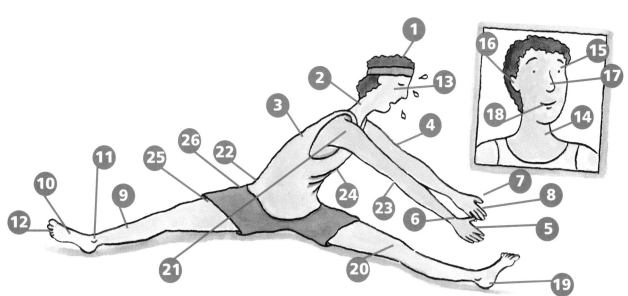

C. GROUP WORK Have you ever had a problem with, hurt, or broken any part of your body? Tell your classmates about the problem, what happened, and what you did to get better.

palm = the inner surface of your hands, not including your fingers

Stiff neck? Try yoga!

Alan has been traveling a lot. He's staying in a hostel in Bangkok, where he has made friends with another American tourist.

A. Listen and practice.

Alan: Ooh! I'm not used to so much traveling. My neck is aching.

Sara: You should take up yoga.

Alan: How would that help?

Sara: Well, yoga relaxes your muscles and, in general, it helps you take better care of yourself.

Alan: Okay, then. Show me a yoga exercise for a stiff neck.

Sara: Sure. Watch this. Stand with your feet apart, and hands behind your back. With palms facing upwards, hold a pole or an umbrella, and bend forward. Bring your hands up and over as far as you can. Hold the posture for 10–20 seconds.

Alan: That looks easy enough.

Sara: It is. Try it. Here's the umbrella.

Alan: Aw!

Sara: Oh, no! Did you hurt yourself?

Alan: No, but I don't think I'll take up yoga.

Sara: Don't be silly. You'll get used to the postures soon enough if you practice.

Alan: Yeah, I think I'll pass.

B. PAIR WORK Discuss why Alan's neck hurts. What does Sara do to avoid problems with her health in general? Why does Alan decide that yoga is not for him?

CULTURE UP CLOSE

Yoga has been practiced in India for over two millennia and is one of India's greatest gifts to humankind. It takes care of both physical and mental health and is considered a philosophy, a science, and an art. The word *yoga* comes from the Sanskrit root *yuj* meaning to join or yoke and implies the joining of every aspect of a human being from the innermost to the external. As a philosophy, yoga is unusual, as it insists that the practice of postures—physical exercises—and breathing techniques is essential in order to lead a good and satisfying life. Yoga is now practiced all over the world, and people in many countries find it helps them fight stress.

posture = specific physical position

GROUP WORK Is yoga popular in your country? Do you practice it? Would you? Give your reasons.

3 Grammar in Context

Talking about new and established routines

To get used to		
to get	**used to**	**noun/gerund**
Alan is **getting**		long-distance travel.
In England, he **got**	**used to**	drinking a lot of tea.
How did you **get**		living here?

To get used to means to adapt to something or someone.
Get used to can be followed by a noun, pronoun, or gerund.
When you conjugate the verb *get, used to* always remains the same.
Don't forget: the *d* of *used* and the *t* of *to* become one sound /t/.

To be used to		
to be	**used to**	**noun/gerund**
Sara is		long-distance travel.
Alan fell over because he **isn't**	**used to**	doing yoga.
Neither Sara nor Alan **was**		Asian food but now they love it.

Be used to means that someone has adapted to something or someone.
Like *get used to*, *be used to* can be followed by a noun, pronoun, or gerund.
When you work with the verb *be, used to* always remains the same.

Practice

A. GROUP WORK Brainstorm with your classmates all the things you have to get used to in the following situations.

Example: You go to live in a foreign country.
If you go to live in a foreign country, you have to get used to the food.

1. You go to live in a foreign country.

2. You start a new English course.

3. You take up a new sport, e.g., golf.

4. You become a parent for the first time.

5. You have just gotten married.

6. You have just moved to a new house.

Interact

B. **PAIR WORK** First work alone and complete the following statements with true information. Then interview your partner to find out about him or her.

Example: What are you used to doing first thing in the morning?
I'm used to drinking a cup of strong tea.

1. First thing in the morning, I am used to _____.

2. Even if I lived to be 100, I could never get used to _____.

3. If I go and live abroad, I know I will find it hard to get used to _____.

4. In English, I am still not used to _____.

5. I used to hate _____, but then I got used to it.

4 Grammar in Context

Talking about self-directed actions

Reflexive Pronouns		
Subject pronoun	**Verb/action**	**Reflexive pronoun**
I	cut	**myself** shaving this morning
Alan	didn't hurt	**himself** doing yoga.
Have you ever	taught	**yourself** how to do something?
We	enjoyed	**ourselves** at the party last night.
Julie never	talks to	**herself** but Greg does.
Travelers often	don't take care of	**themselves** on long trips.
The situation	speaks for	**itself.** There's a serious drought here.

Use reflexive pronouns
- when the subject and direct object refer to the same person or thing.
- after prepositions only when it is not clear who or what the object is.

Contrast: **She was talking to *herself*** with **She was talking to us/them/me, etc.**
          BUT **He went for a walk and took the dog with him.**

It is clear that the dog is going for a walk with him so the reflexive is not necessary.

- as part of the subject of the sentence for emphasis.

The director *himself* admits that business is not very good at the moment.

In this case, the reflexive can be placed after the clause in which it occurs to emphasize that someone did something instead of or without the help of others.

Examples: **Since Jenny didn't want to do it, I spoke to the manager *myself*.**
          OR **Thanks for offering to help, but I can do it *myself*.**

Practice

A. PAIR WORK **Complete the dialogs with reflexive pronouns.**

1. A: How would you describe _____?

 B: Well, first, I would describe _____ as cheerful and outgoing.

2. A: Do you ever talk to _____?

 B: No, but my father talks to _____ all the time. He's so funny.

3. A: What about your mother? Does she talk to _____?

 B: No, but she's funny, too. She's always trying to teach _____ something new.

4. A: Do your parents enjoy _____ now that they are retired?

 B: Oh, yes. And they take very good care of _____. They do yoga every day and eat a very healthy diet.

5. A: They're lucky. I don't have the time to take good care of _____.

 B: That's too bad. We should all make the time to take good care of _____.

Interact

B. GROUP WORK **First work alone and complete the following statements with true information.**

Example: I'd describe myself as _____.
 I'd describe myself as hardworking and very funny.

1. I would describe myself as _____.

2. When I was a child, I taught myself to _____.

3. I enjoy myself by _____.

4. Recently, I hurt myself when I _____.

5. I talk to myself when _____.

Pronunciation

C. Listen and repeat.

1. The president himself came to see us.

2. If you don't call him, I'll do it myself.

3. Adam's group left early, so he finished the job himself.

D. PAIR WORK **Take turns reading the sentences aloud.**

1. Nick himself admits that Julie is a brilliant table tennis player.

2. The government itself does not know what to do about the economic crisis.

3. The children wrote the letters to their grandparents themselves.

4. Mike can't help us so we will simply have to do all the work ourselves.

5. Okay, forget it! I'll do it myself.

5 Vocabulary in Context

Talking about aches, pains, and injuries

LANGUAGE UP CLOSE

ache (n) = a constant but not very serious pain. It combines with these body parts: *head, stomach, ear, back, tooth.* For example, *stomachache.* Verb = *to ache*

One of the advantages of a yoga program is that it makes your body very flexible because you **stretch, bend,** and **extend** it a lot when doing yoga postures.

If you practice yoga, you will find that it helps **cure** a lot of aches and pains.

But if you **burn, break,** or **sprain** a part of your body, yoga cannot **heal** these **injuries.** You will have to get help from a doctor.

Yoga can, however, help with the healing process by training the **injured** person to relax mentally and emotionally. This strengthens their **immune system** and accelerates the healing process.

Practice

A. **Complete the text with one of the words in boldface above, or a derivative of one of these words.**

A: Hey, have you heard? Pete _____ his arm at training this morning.

B: Oh, no! How long will it take to _____?

A: I'm not sure—about 6 weeks I think. Oh, yeah, and Alex _____ his ankle.

B: You're kidding! We've had so much bad luck! Hey, take care of yourself the next few days. We don't want any more _____ on our team.

A: Don't worry about me. I'm very careful, and I have a wonderful _____.

B: Yeah, I've noticed. You're hardly ever sick, are you?

A: I go to yoga twice a week and I think it _____ a lot of my aches and pains, and keeps my immune system healthy.

B: Yeah, and all the _____ and _____ keeps you flexible, too.

A: Yes, and yoga keeps me cheerful—even when every player on our team seems to be _____!

 **Interact**

B. **PAIR WORK** First work alone and think of the last time you
hurt, injured, cut, and burned yourself and be prepared to tell
your partner all the details.

Example: S1: *When I was cooking dinner last weekend, I burned myself.*
S2: *Oh, no! What happened?*
S1: *Well, I was getting something out of the oven and I burned my hand on the
oven door.*
S2: *That's too bad. I hope it heals quickly.*

Tell the class what you learned about your partner.

Example: *Sara burned herself when she was cooking last weekend.*
She was getting . . . etc.

> *painkiller =*
> *medicine to*
> *stop pain*

6 Listening in Context

Focus Strategy: Identifying speakers

Before you listen

A. **GROUP WORK** Discuss the emergency remedies
your family has for these problems: *stomachache,
headache, toothache, backache, earache.*

First listening

B. **Listen and complete columns 1 and 2. Choose
the participants from this list:** *mother and daughter;
husband and wife; boss and employee; coach and athlete;
doctor and patient.*

	Participants	Ache	Solution	Advice
1.				
2.				
3.				
4.				
5.				

Second listening

C. **PAIR WORK** Listen again and complete the remaining columns.
Share your answers with your partner, and add any extra
information from his or her notes to yours.

Reading

Focus Strategy: Outlining for comprehension

READING UP CLOSE

While reading, make a mental outline of the text. Use parallel concepts to better understand the text.

Before you read

A. GROUP WORK How common is make-up use? If you are a woman do you yourself wear make-up? If you are a man, do the women in your family or your women friends wear it? Why do you think many women like to use make-up? What are some possible reasons why others do not?

While you read

B. Skim the text and decide:

1. Which two groups of women does the text talk about?
2. What does Victoria Jackson do to try to help them?
3. Has Victoria's work been successful or unsuccessful?

make-up = cosmetics used on the face; such as lipstick, mascara, powder

Look Good, Feel Better

Make-up and self esteem can make an interesting partnership for women cancer patients and prisoners. Both groups commonly suffer from a loss of confidence because of the conditions of their lives. Women who have cancer often lose their hair and put on or lose a lot of weight because of the medications they take, so in general they do not feel very good about themselves. These women may be used to feeling in control, but they can lose this confidence when the process of coping with cancer takes over their lives completely. Women who are in prison have also lost control of their lives and may feel unloved and unlovable because of where they are. They often believe that, once they leave prison, the world will be a cruel and unwelcoming place, so they develop a hard image of themselves to try and hide their true feelings.

Over the past twenty years, however, women cancer patients and women prisoners have received a lot of help with these problems, thanks to the work of an expert make-up artist named Victoria Jackson. Victoria runs make-up seminars in prisons and clinics such as the Twin Towers Correctional Facilities and Cedars-Sinai Comprehensive Cancer Center in Los Angeles. She believes that, if women prisoners use make-up to soften their image, they will feel better about themselves and this will have a positive effect on people's attitudes toward them when they leave prison.

While the prisoners learn to use make-up as an aid to believe in themselves, the cancer patients use the make-up routine to regain some normality in their lives. "There are few moments in the day," says Victoria, "when we can concentrate so completely on ourselves." The application of make-up gives cancer patients a focused routine to cope with who they are.

Big cosmetic companies support work like Victoria's by providing free cosmetics for the make-up seminars, and seminars like these are now organized in many countries. After a seminar, there is a total transformation in the women; they walk out with heads high, looking really wonderful—and feeling so much better about themselves.

After you read

C. **GROUP WORK** First, read the text alone. Then with the other students in your group, fill in the outline information about Victoria's seminars.

1. Seminar leader: _____ .

2. Seminar participants: (a) _____ (b) _____ .

3. General aim of seminars: _____ .

4. Problems participants have: _____
   _____ .

5. Specific aims of seminars: _____ .

6. Reasons for success of seminars: _____ .

D. **GROUP WORK** If you were in charge of a women's prison or a cancer clinic, would you organize make-up seminars? Why or why not? After reading this article have your opinions about make-up changed? If so, how?

 **Writing**

Focus Strategy: Outlining

 **WRITING UP CLOSE**

Using an outline to produce a written text helps to produce a logical, organized piece of work. This will make the text easier to understand.

Before you write

A. **GROUP WORK** Discuss other seminars or support programs that could help cancer patients or people in prison.

 Write

B. **PAIR WORK** Write an outline for one of the seminars you brainstormed in A. Imagine you are going to send it to the person in charge of a prison or cancer clinic. Use this structure:

Seminar title: _____

Problems participants have: _____

Seminar participants: _____

Specific aims of seminar: _____

General aim of seminar: _____

Support needed for seminar: _____

C. Join another pair. Read and comment on each other's proposals.

9 Putting It Together

A. PAIR WORK Play the *'I know, but . . .'* game. Brainstorm with your partner a common problem.

Example: *stomachache, headache, low self-esteem, depression*

Choose one of these problems. Student 1 takes the role of a person with the problem and Student 2 the role of a person who is giving him or her advice. Every time, Student 2 gives Student 1 advice he or she rejects it with *I know, but . . .* + a reason for not accepting the advice. The person who cannot think of anything to say loses.

Example: the problem = stomachache

Student 1: *Oh, no. I've got a stomachache again.*

Student 2: *Well, let's face it. You don't take very good care of yourself, do you? You eat too much.*

Student 1: ***I know, but*** *I work hard, and I'd get weak if I ate less.*

Student 2: *No, you wouldn't. You'd get used to it. And another problem is you eat too much fast food. You should eat at home more often.*

Student 1: ***I know, but*** *I live alone and I don't know how to cook for myself.*

Student 2: *You can learn. It's easy.*

Student 1: ***I know, but*** *I don't have the time. I work late and . . .*

Change roles and problems and play the game again.

B. PAIR WORK Find a partner with different problems from the ones you had in A and play the game again.

Stay TUNED

Credit Card Applications

STAY TUNED "You could charge it on your credit card, couldn't you?"

Cash or charge?

Communication	Grammar	Vocabulary	Skills
Asking for agreement and confirmation	Tag questions with *could, would, should, can,* and *will*	Money matters	Listening to a radio report
Expressing surprise and determination	Use of *still* with *be* and other verbs	*To be in debt*	Reading a newspaper article
Making decisions about money matters		*To get into debt*	Writing a newspaper article
		Hold on a minute.	
		That's a lot.	
		I can't wait to see that.	
		Phrasal verbs	

currency = the money specific to one country

1 Warm Up

A. PAIR WORK Label the pictures using the vocabulary below.

coin	dollar bill	traveler's check	credit card	store credit card	bank statement

B. PAIR WORK Work with a partner and discuss the kinds of coins and bills in your currency.

> Example: *In our currency, we have a ten-cent coin; a fifty-cent coin; a twenty-peso bill, etc.*

C. Listen and circle the currencies you hear.

yen	pound sterling
euro	U.S. dollar
won	Mexican peso
real	Taiwanese dollar

CULTURE UP CLOSE

The euro is a new currency. It is used within the EU (Union of European States) and has replaced the currencies of most of the countries in the union; for example, it has replaced the French franc, German Mark, Italian lira, Spanish peseta, etc.

D. GROUP WORK Discuss the currencies in C. How much are they worth compared to the currency in your country? Where can you find this information?

I'm working on getting rich.

Mike and Nick are walking down the street on their way to Café Puro.

A. **Listen and practice.**

Mike: Hold on a minute. I want to check out that digital camera.

Nick: Sure, I'll go in with you. Wow, look at the price. It's almost $300. That's a lot.

Mike: I know. I can't even afford Julie's good-bye present.

Nick: Well, you could charge the camera on your credit card, couldn't you?

Mike: No, I'll just wait and save some money first. I don't need any more debt. I'm still paying back my student loans.

Nick: Really? I paid mine off last month. I'm glad to have that over with.

Mike: Well, I'll have mine paid off sometime soon. So, what are you going to do now that you're out of debt?

Nick: I don't know. Maybe I'll start working on getting rich.

B. **PAIR WORK** **Discuss why Mike doesn't buy the digital camera. How serious do you think Nick is about his future plans? Explain your answers.**

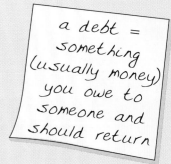

a debt = something (usually money) you owe to someone and should return

C ULTURE UP CLOSE

In the United States, many students do not have enough money to pay tuition and support themselves while they go to school. Some take out student loans to pay for the things they need, with the idea that they will repay the loan when they finish college and have a well-paying job. This type of loan is available through government programs and sometimes in local banks.

GROUP WORK **Do you think taking out student loans is a good practice? Give your reasons. Are there similar programs in your country?**

3 Grammar in Context

Asking for agreement and confirmation

Tag questions with modal auxiliaries	
Affirmative main clause	**Negative tag**
This **would** be a good present, You **could** charge it on your credit card, We **should** try to spend less money on fast food,	**wouldn't** it? **couldn't** you? **shouldn't** we?
Negative main clause	**Positive tag**
We **shouldn't** spend so much on clothes, Nick **won't** get into debt again, Alan **can't** afford to stay in expensive hotels,	**should** we? **will** he? **can** he?

- Use tag questions to ask for confirmation of what you are saying. A falling tag indicates that you are sure of your facts and expect the other person to agree. A rising tag indicates that you are not sure and are asking for the facts.
- When the main clause is in the positive form, the tag is negative. When the main clause is in the negative form, the tag is positive.

Practice

A. PAIR WORK First read the dialogs alone. Then work with your partner and complete the dialogs with the correct tag question. Act out the dialogs.

1. **A:** We could go to the movies tonight, _____?

   B: Yeah, but we won't save any money if we go out so much, _____?

2. **A:** Nick will be at Julie's farewell party, _____?

   B: I hope so. It would look bad if he didn't come, _____?

3. **A:** I can't seem to save any money these days, _____?

   B: No, you can't. You won't find it easy to pay off all your debt, _____?

4. **A:** I'd look good in that shirt, _____?

   B: Well, you really shouldn't spend any more money today, _____?

Interact

B. PAIR WORK Take turns being the people in the following situations and giving each other advice using a modal auxiliary and tag question.

Example: to be broke
   S1: *I'm broke.*
   S2: *That's too bad. You **could** spend less money on traveling, **couldn't you?***

1. to be broke
2. to be putting on weight
3. to feel tired all the time
4. to have a vacation next month
5. to have a free international airline ticket
6. to have visitors next week

4 Grammar in Context

Expressing surprise and determination

Still + be and + continuous forms

Where's Casey?	She's **still** in the library.
Why is Mike always so broke?	He's **still** paying off his student loans.
Is Julie still at work?	Yeah, when I left she was **still** in the office.
Why are you late?	I overslept. I was **still** sleeping at 9 A.M.

Use **still** to show that you are surprised that an activity or situation is continuing and you expected it to finish earlier or to emphasize the fact that the activity is continuing.

Still + other verb forms

Why are you always saving money?	Because I **still** haven't paid off my bank loans.
How's the new student?	Okay, but she **still** seems pretty shy.
Are you going to study after class?	Yeah, I **still** don't understand tag questions.
Do you remember where we were this time last year?	Yeah, I **can still** remember where we were.

With verbs other than **be,** continue to use **still** to express surprise and also to insist that something has not finished. Place **still** between the subject and the verb except when there is a positive modal auxiliary. **I can still remember where we were when. . . .**

Practice

A. **PAIR WORK** With your partner, rewrite these sentences, adding *still*.

Example: Even if we went on vacation, we might be
able to afford a new car.
Even if we went on vacation, we might still be
able to afford a new car.

I still have my first soccer trophy.

1. Oh, no! It is dark, and we will have to go to work soon.

2. Does your sister work in the evenings?

3. Are you repaying a student loan?

4. It's 5 o'clock already, and I haven't finished all my work.

5. Mike can't believe the news about Casey.

6. We've saved so much this year, but we don't have enough money to buy a car.

7. Alan is in Japan, but he leaves for Los Angeles on Saturday.

8. The U.S. dollar is one of the strongest currencies in the world.

9. Nick doesn't know what he is going to do with his extra money.

10. Julie can beat Nick at table tennis without any difficulty.

Interact

B. GROUP WORK Discuss things in your own life or in your country that you find surprising because they are still happening or still true.

Example: *We still have a picture of Simon Bolivar on our one thousand-peso bills.*
My whole family still gets together for a party on New Year's Eve.

5 Vocabulary in Context

Talking about money and money matters

If you pay for a purchase with coins or bills then you are **paying cash.** You can also often write out a check. If you pay with your credit card, then you are **charging** it.

If you pay for something with cash and need money back, the money returned to you is the **change.** Often in a bar or café you will hear a customer say to a waiter **"Keep the change."** So the change becomes the waiter's **tip.** In general, a tip is 15–20 percent of the bill.

In some restaurants and hotels, the tip is called the **service charge** and is usually included automatically in the total amount to be paid. In some countries, **taxes** are also added—both in stores and in restaurants.

If you **borrow** money (from a bank or another person), that money is called **a loan.** You normally repay a bank loan in monthly **installments.**

The money you earn on a monthly or weekly basis is your **income.** If you are unable to immediately repay money you owe from your income, you are **in debt.**

At a bank you keep your money in an **account,** and the bank sends you **statements** to show what has gone into and out of the account. The **balance** is the money left in the account when the statement is sent.

Practice

A. **Read the explanations below and find a matching word or expression from the texts above:**

1. The money I owe to a bank: _____

2. The extra money I pay in a café or restaurant to the waiter: _____

3. The money left in my account at the end of the month: _____

4. The money I pay every month to repay a loan: _____

5. The extra money I pay in a store which goes to the government: _____

6. My situation if I cannot repay the money I owe: _____

7. The money I get back when I make a small payment from a large bill: _____

8. The place where I keep my money in a bank: _____

9. The money I earn or receive to live on: _____

10. The bank's record of the money that goes into and out of my account: _____

Phrasal Verbs

Multiple-part or phrasal verbs consist of a verb + one or more small parts (particles), which look like prepositions and/or adverbs. There are three groups of phrasal verbs.

1. Phrasal verbs that never take an object: *sit down, stand up, watch out, get up, turn up.*

    Guess who *turned up* at the party? John. I haven't seen him in a long time.

2. Phrasal verbs that take an object and particle can go before or after the object when the object is a noun: *pay off/back, throw away, bring up, switch on/off, try on.*

    Nick is happy that he has *paid off* his student loans.
    Nick is happy that he has *paid* his student loans *off*.

When the object of these verbs is a pronoun, the verb and particle must be separate and the particle comes after the pronoun.

Mike is worried about his debt because he still hasn't *paid* it *off*.

B. **Write out and complete the sentences with one of the phrasal verbs from the box above. Put the noun or pronoun in the correct position.**

1. _____. There's a train coming.

2. They borrowed too much money from the bank and still haven't been able to _____ (it).

3. I didn't _____ early this morning. I was too tired.

4. Please, don't _____ (your old clothes.) Send them to a refugee camp.

5. Stacey decided not to _____ (the green skirt) because she knew it was too expensive for her to buy.

Focus Strategy: Identifying points of view

prefunded = the money is already there

to chew out = to speak angrily at someone

Before you listen

A. Do people in your country use credit cards? What do you think of the system of paying by credit card? What are some of the advantages and disadvantages? Do you think it is a good idea for teenagers to have credit cards?

First listening

B. Listen to the radio report. Put a check in column one for the people whose opinions are reported. In the second column, indicate with *F* if they are for and *A* if they are against credit cards for teenagers.

✔	F/A	People interviewed	Reason
		A psychiatrist	
✓	F	A teenage girl	Makes her feel older
		A father	
		A teenage boy	
		A mother	
		A high school teacher	
		A second teenage girl	
		A representative of a credit card company	
		A representative of a debt organization	

Second listening

C. **PAIR WORK** Listen again and write notes to complete column 4 with at least one reason for each of the people's opinions you checked in B. Share your notes with your partner and add information from his or her notes to yours.

CULTURE UP CLOSE

In the year 2000 alone, U.S. citizens added 1,400 billion dollars to their personal debts.

7 Reading

Focus Strategy: Inferring

READING UP CLOSE

Sometimes when you read, you have to guess the meaning of some of the words in the text. When you do this, use the other information in the text to help you to guess what the words mean. It is also a good idea to use any knowledge you already have of the subject matter to help you understand new words.

Before you read

A. Do you know what these people have in common: *Bill Gates, Paloma Picasso, King Fahd of Saudi Arabia,* and *Sam Robson Walton?* Do you know the names of any very rich people in your region or country? How did they make their money? Do they use some of their money to help your community? If so, what do they do?

While you read

B. Read the text about Sam Robson Walton, Jr., one of the richest people in the world, and check the phrases that you think describe him well.

_____ a very private person   _____ a person who learned a lot from his father

_____ a very selfish person   _____ a person who spends his money foolishly

_____ a very wise person   _____ a person who shares his money with the community

Sam the Invisible Man

One of the richest men in the world **inherited** two things from his father: billions of dollars and a dislike of publicity. Sam Robson Walton is chairperson of Wal-Mart, the world's biggest retailer, but if you log onto Wal-Mart's website, there is no picture of him. He and his family like a quiet life and live **anonymously** in their unostentatious home in Arkansas.

It is easy to understand why Robson Walton avoids publicity. When his father— also called Sam—**founded** Wal-Mart in 1961and became the richest man in the world, he had a bad experience with the **media.** They claimed he was cheap, and eccentric. Stories appeared in newspapers and on the radio and TV saying, among other things, that Sam still slept with his dogs. Although this was probably an **exaggeration,** there appears to be some truth to the fact that, even after he became rich, Sam Robson Walton, Sr., continued to drive a very old pick-up truck, had five-dollar haircuts at the local barber shop, and was notorious for never leaving a tip.

Sam Robson Walton, Sr., soon believed that if he told the media too much about himself, they would **ruin** his life. So he taught his son at an early age how to avoid problems with publicity. Wal-Mart, which started with only one small store and now has more than 4,000 stores across the world, never reveals personal information about its boss. A spokesperson for Wal-Mart recently claimed that *Where does he live?, Does he travel much?* and *Does he own a yacht?* are personal questions, and Wal-Mart answers only questions about the Wal-Mart business. So, today Sam Robson Walton, Jr., keeps busy in his Arkansas home, quietly planning how to spend his money, a lot of which he **gives away.** For example, five universities in the United States benefited greatly when they received a total of $20 million dollars from the Wal-Mart Charitable Trust.

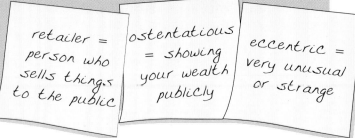

retailer = person who sells things to the public

ostentatious = showing your wealth publicly

eccentric = very unusual or strange

After you read

C. PAIR WORK **Find and discuss the facts which prove that**

1. Sam Robson Walton, Jr., does not like publicity.
2. Sam Robson Walton, Sr., was good at saving money.
3. Wal-Mart respects the privacy of Sam Robson Walton, Jr.
4. Wal-Mart has made a lot of progress since 1961.
5. Sam Robson Walton, Jr., is generous with his money.

D. GROUP WORK **Try to guess the meanings of the words highlighted in boldface in the reading.**

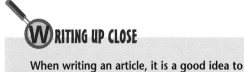

WRITING UP CLOSE

When writing an article, it is a good idea to choose a topic you are familiar with or that interests you. This will make your writing more interesting and factual.

8 Writing

Focus Strategy: Writing for human interest

Before you write

A. GROUP WORK **Think of a famous person in your country, or in the history of your country, who was very rich, funny, or artistic and eccentric. Discuss the reasons why he or she was eccentric.**

Write

B. **Write a short newspaper article about this eccentric person. Use this structure:**

Title of article

Name, origins, and age

Examples of eccentric behavior

Your explanation for the eccentric behavior

Professional activities

Personal characteristics

Influence on community

9 Putting It Together

A. PAIR WORK Read through the situation and the cued dialog.

Situation: You and your partner work for the same company. The company has been very successful recently and has paid all its employees an extra month's salary each. This means that you and your partner can spend the sum of two extra month's salary between you. Unfortunately, you can't decide what to do with it.

S1: Suggest that you use the money to pay off one of your loans, a car loan, and indicate that you are sure S2 will agree.

S2: Disagree with S1's suggestion and indicate that the two of you never have any money to spend. Elicit S1's agreement on this. Say that it would be better to spend it on a vacation.

S1: Remind S2 of how much money you owe altogether and express your fear of getting into debt.

S2: Indicate that you think S1 is crazy to worry about getting into debt, as you pay all the installments on your loans regularly. Insist that you believe you both need a vacation and give reasons.

S1: Remind S2 that you know you always make your payments regularly, but that it is always an effort and if you paid off the car loan you would have more money to spend on a weekly basis and could relax at home. Indicate that you expect S2 to agree with this argument.

S2: Indicate that you have not changed your opinion of what you want to do, and suggest that you both think about it and discuss it again tomorrow.

S1: Agree to this suggestion.

B. PAIR WORK Calculate how much two medium-income monthly salaries would be in your own currency. Then take turns at being student 1 and student 2 and at acting out the dialog. Use your own currency in any calculations you make.

C. GROUP WORK Join another pair of students and listen as you each act out the dialog again. Then discuss what you would do if you really were in this situation. Which of you are the big savers and which are the big spenders?

Stay TUNED

 STAY TUNED Where is Casey going?

Keep in touch.

Communication	Grammar	Vocabulary	Skills
Highlighting information	*How* + adverb/adjective	Farewells	Listening to short informal speeches
Checking travel arrangements	Tag questions with present perfect	Paying compliments	Reading song lyrics
Giving short informal speeches		*On behalf of* . . .	Writing short farewell speeches
		For my part . . .	
		Phrasal verbs	

1 Warm Up

A. PAIR WORK Complete the farewell greetings with the words and expressions below.

Good _____!

All the _____!

_____ when you get on-line.

Keep _____.

Have a good _____!

Take _____.

Thanks for all your _____.

Come and _____ sometime.

_____ in L.A.!

hospitality   best   visit me   care   in touch   see you   luck   trip   e-mail

B. Listen and decide.

1. Who is saying good-bye to whom?
2. Where are they?
3. Where and when might they meet again?

C. GROUP WORK When did you last say good-bye to someone you love? Did you say good-bye at a bus station, a train station, an airport, or a seaport? How did you feel? Have you kept in touch with that person? How? If you went overseas for a long time, would you like your family and friends to come to the airport to say good-bye? Why, or why not?

CULTURE UP CLOSE

In Japan, someone who is going away may receive a gift of origami cranes. The crane represents great fortune, and one thousand origami cranes is a traditional symbol of health, peace, and even fertility. Making a gift of origami cranes is a way to wish a traveler all the blessings of good fortune.

2 Conversation

A farewell party

Julie is returning to Korea. Her co-workers at WebWorld have organized a farewell office party. Greg is making a farewell speech.

A. Listen and practice.

Greg: Julie, I'd like to thank you on behalf of everyone for your excellent contribution to WebWorld. You've been a fun, creative, hardworking colleague! You can't imagine how much we've enjoyed working with you. We'll miss you a lot, and we hope you will keep in touch. Please accept this small present as an expression of our admiration and friendship.

Julie: Thank you, Greg, and thank you everybody for your good wishes and for the present. For my part, I'd just like to say how happy I've been working with you all. It's been a big challenge but we've been a great team and I've learned a lot. I'll be sure to write—and you've all got my e-mail! . . . Oh, thank you! The gift is beautiful—and very appropriate.

B. PAIR WORK Why did Julie's co-workers enjoy working with her? Why did Julie enjoy working at WebWorld? How is Julie planning to stay in touch with her WebWorld colleagues?

CULTURE UP CLOSE

When a person leaves a job, it is customary, in most English-speaking countries, for his or her colleagues to buy him or her a present and to organize a small party, at which a boss or manager may give a short farewell speech. The person who is leaving often responds with his or her own farewell speech. Then, he or she opens the present and shows it to everyone and thanks colleagues again.

GROUP WORK What kind of customs do you have in your country when a co-worker resigns from his or her job? If you organize a farewell party, do you have it at the office or do you go to a restaurant? What kind of things do you give as farewell presents?

3 Grammar in Context

Highlighting information

How + adverb/adjective	
Direct speech form	**Indirect speech form**
We've enjoyed working with you **so/very much.**	You can't imagine **how much** we've enjoyed working with you.
They've all worked **so/very hard.**	Let me remind you **how hard** they have all worked.
It took Casey **a long time** to get her visas.	Casey can't believe **how long** it took to get her visas.
Time has gone **so/very quickly** since Casey decided to volunteer abroad.	You've no idea **how quickly** time has passed since Casey decided to volunteer abroad.
I've been very **happy** here.	I'd like to say **how happy** I've been here.
This experience has been **wonderful.**	You can't imagine **how wonderful** this experience has been.
You were so **tired.**	I'm sorry. We didn't realize **how tired** you were.

Highlight information by expressing it in indirect speech with the help of expressions such as: ***can't believe, have no idea, remind, can't imagine.*** Use ***how*** + adv. or ***how*** + adj. from the original direct speech form to introduce the indirect speech version.

Pronunciation

A. Listen and repeat the indirect statements in the box above.

B. **PAIR WORK** Listen to the following statements. Where is the stress in each statement? Underline the stressed word or words. Discuss your answers with your partner.

1. You've no idea how long I've been waiting for you.
2. I can just imagine how tired Casey must be feeling after all that packing.
3. Let me remind you how careful you should be when you travel alone.
4. We can't believe how much we have learned from this book.

C. Listen again and repeat.

Practice

D. Highlight the information in the following statements by expressing them in indirect form.

1. The airport is very busy these days.
2. The flight is late leaving.
3. It took Julie a long time to pack.
4. Casey is excited about her project.
5. Julie enjoyed working here very much.
6. The employees are working hard.
7. The flight is very long.
8. Julie is sad to be leaving.
9. Jason is nervous about Casey's work.
10. Alan has traveled a lot this month.

Grammar in Context

Checking travel arrangements

Tag questions with present perfect

Positive statement	Negative tag
You've confirmed your departure time,	haven't you?
Julie has finished packing	hasn't she?
We've labeled the baggage,	haven't we?

Negative statement	Positive tag
Nick and Julie haven't had their last table tennis game,	have they?
I haven't forgotten anything,	have I?
Alan hasn't arrived back in L.A. yet,	has he?

Use tag questions with the present perfect to check actions and states which are relevant to the present or to the recent or immediate past.

Practice

A. PAIR WORK Work alone and check in column 1 for the things you would do first when preparing for a long international trip. Put an *X* for the ones you would leave till the last minute.

Me	My partner	Things to do for my trip
		get all the visas I need
		get all the necessary vaccinations
		pack my suitcase
		check the departure time for the flight
		book my ticket
		buy some books to read during the journey
		call a taxi to take me to the airport.
		make a hotel reservation in the city I will be flying to

Now, ask your partner which arrangements he or she would make first, and check those items in the second column of the chart. Imagine you really are preparing for a trip, and ask each other questions about the arrangements you have already made.

B. Use the information in the table in A to report information to the class.

Example: *Makiko has gotten all her visas, but she hasn't packed her suitcases yet.*

5 Vocabulary in Context

Paying compliments

A lot of people in L.A. will be sad to see Casey leave. She is a **warm, generous,** and **caring** friend.

At WebWorld, people are sorry to see Julie leave. She has been a **fun, creative,** and **hardworking** colleague.

At the office or in our personal lives, we like to have colleagues or friends who are **trustworthy, reliable,** and **supportive.**

Practice

A. **Use one adjective from the texts above for the people described in the sentences.**

1. I can tell Ken all my secrets. He never tells them to anyone else. _____

2. If Alan promises to do something, he always does it. He never forgets. _____

3. Mike works from 9 to 5 every day, and takes a very short break for lunch. _____

4. Julie always organizes the best parties. _____

5. Casey is always prepared to listen when someone is sick, depressed, or worried. _____

6. At WebWorld, colleagues work together to help solve major problems. _____

7. Nick is not very hardworking but he always has new and unusual ideas. _____

8. Stacey never complains if she has to do extra housework while Casey is studying for her exams. _____

Word formation

Adjectives that end in the suffix *-ive* or *-ative* have usually been formed from verbs. Look at the example and then complete the verb column in the chart.

Example: *creative (adj.) to create (v)*
            talkative (adj.) to talk (v)

Verb	Adjective
1. _____	productive
2. _____	attractive
3. _____	imaginative
4. _____	informative
5. _____	appreciative

Phrasal Verbs

Some Phrasal Verbs always take an object (noun or pronoun) and the object must always go immediately after the particle; in other words, the verb and particle cannot be separated. This group includes phrasal verbs with more than one particle: **ask for, look after, get over, stand by, look forward to, get along with, stand up for.**

Jan is in bed. She still hasn't gotten over the flu.
I'm looking forward to Julie's farewell party. Nick is looking forward to it, too.

B. PAIR WORK Complete the interactions with one of the verbs in the box above.

1. **A:** Excuse me, you've forgotten to bring my coffee.

   B: I'm so sorry. Did you _____ coffee?

2. **A:** Can you _____ my grandfather when I go away?

   B: Of course, I enjoy the company of older people.

3. **A:** Is Casey leaving this week?

   B: Yes, and she is _____ the new experience very much.

4. **A:** I think Jason has been great about all this.

   B: Yes, it is good to see that he has _____ Casey.

5. **A:** Julie is sad to say good-bye, isn't she?

   B: Yes, she's even sorry to say good-bye to Greg. At first, she didn't _____ him, but now she likes him a lot.

C. Many phrasal verbs can be replaced by one-word verbs. Phrasal verbs are considered less formal than one-word verbs. Rewrite the sentences below, replacing the one-word verbs with the correct form of one of the phrasal verbs in this list.

	Less Formal	Formal
Example:	*Julie knows how* **to stand up for** *herself.* =	*Julie knows how to* **defend** *herself.*

put off	turn up	pay back	fall out	break up

1. The company director has just **arrived** and we weren't expecting him till next week.

2. Could you please **postpone** the meeting until next week? I won't be here tomorrow.

3. Are you still **repaying** that loan?

4. Ana has **finished her relationship** with Paul.

5. They **quarreled** a week ago.

6 Listening in Context

Focus Strategy: Listening for specific information

LISTENING UP CLOSE

Listening to a text more than once allows you to identify information you might not have understood the first time. Be sure to concentrate every time you listen.

Before you listen

A. You will hear Alan say good-bye to Toshio and his parents and Casey say good-bye to her friends in L.A. Do you think these farewells will be happy, sad, or a little bit of both? Give reasons for your predictions.

First listening

B. Listen and decide.

1. Is Alan's farewell happy, sad, or both? _____

2. Where are Alan's Japanese friends saying good-bye to him? _____

3. Is Casey's farewell happy, sad, or both? _____

4. Where are Casey's friends saying good-bye to her? _____

5. Whose speech do you hear from Alan's farewell? _____

Second listening

C. PAIR WORK **Listen again. First work alone and complete the notes. Then compare your notes with your partner's.**

1. Personal qualities of Alan's Japanese friends: _____

2. Arrangements Alan makes to keep in touch with them: _____

3. Reasons why Alan's farewell is both happy and sad: _____

4. Personal qualities of Casey's friends: _____

5. Arrangements Casey makes for keeping in touch with them: _____

6. Reasons why Casey's farewell is both happy and sad: _____

7 Reading

Focus Strategy: Skimming a text for general information

READING UP CLOSE

The lyrics (words) to a song often appear in a different order than they do in normal spoken or written English. The author does this in order to help create the rhyme and the rhythm of the song. When you read lyrics, read an entire verse together. Do not read line by line.

Before you read

A. Do you know the names of any folk songs about farewells in your own language? Are they sad or happy? Are they connected to any specific people or places?

While you read

B. Skim the text of this folk song and decide:

1. What is the occupation of the person who is singing the song?
2. Where is this person traveling to?
3. Where is he traveling from?
4. How many verses are there in the song?
5. How many times is the chorus sung?

The Leaving of Liverpool

1.
Farewell to you, my own true love,
I am going far, far away
I am bound for Californiay,
And I know that I'll return someday

Chorus
So fare thee well, my own true love,
For when I return, united we will be
It's not the leaving of Liverpool that grieves me,
But my darling when I think of thee

2.
I have shipped on a Yankee sailing ship,
Davy Crockett is her name,
And her Captain's name was Burgess,
And they say that she's a floating shame.

Chorus

3.
It's me second trip with Burgess on the Crocket,
And I think I know him well.
If a man's a seaman he'll get along,
But if not then he's sure in hell.

Chorus

4.
Oh, the sun is on the harbour, love,
And I wish that I could remain,
For I know that it will be a long, long time,
Before I see you again.

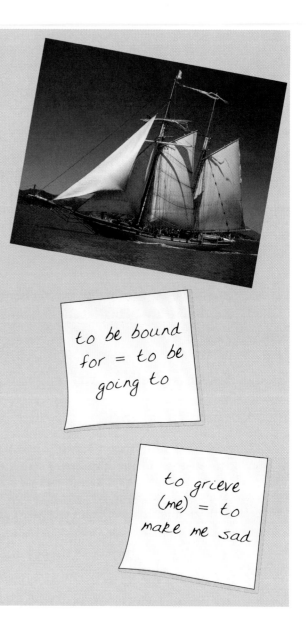

to be bound for = to be going to

to grieve (me) = to make me sad

After you read

C. PAIR WORK Take turns. Read the song again to find these specific facts:

1. The place where the sailor is going: _____

2. The name of the ship the sailor will be working on: _____

3. The name of the captain of the ship: _____

4. The place that the sailor is leaving: _____

D. PAIR WORK Discuss these questions with your partner.

1. How do we know the sailor knows Burgess?
2. How do we know that the journey to California is going to be very hard?
3. What is the main reason the sailor is feeling very sad?
4. What do you think he does to make himself feel happy when he is at sea?
5. Are there any songs in your language which are similar to this one?

8 Writing

Focus Strategy: Writing a farewell speech

WRITING UP CLOSE

When preparing an oral text, such as a speech, you must use language that is appropriate to the task, the context, and the situation.

Before you write

A. GROUP WORK Imagine that you are going to say good-bye to someone you all know well. It could be *a teacher, a classmate from another group; a coworker,* or *a friend who does not study English with you.* Write notes to complete the outline about this person.

Relationship to you: ———————— *friend/colleague/teacher, etc.* ————————

Length of time you have known/worked with him or her: ————————————

Qualities you admire in him or her as a friend/colleague/teacher, etc. ————————

Examples of good things he or she has done as a friend/colleague/teacher etc.: ————

Plans for keeping in touch with him or her: ————————————————

Write

B. PAIR WORK Use the notes in A to write a speech for a farewell party for this person. Look again at the speech in the Conversation on page 112.

C. GROUP WORK Join another pair and take turns reading your speech to the other pair of students and commenting on one another's speeches. Then try giving the speech without reading it. Decide which of you can give the best speech.

D. Choose the best person in your group to give the speech in front of the entire class. After all of the groups have given a speech, the entire class will choose which speech was the best.

9 Putting It Together

GROUP WORK Imagine you have a budget for a farewell party for everyone in your class, and for 6 special guests. The six special guests must be: (a) two famous people from your country; (b) two world-famous people who are not from your country; and (c) two of the *Up Close* characters in Book 4.

- **Special Guest List 1.** First work with the teacher and the whole class and brainstorm a list of the 6 special guests you would invite and give reasons. Think about what each person could do at the party and about their personal qualities.

- **Change in the situation.** Unfortunately you have just heard that the budget for the party has been drastically reduced and you can now invite only three of the original special guests: one famous person from your country; one world-famous person not from your country; one *Up Close* character from Book 4.

- **Special Guest List 2.** With your partner decide which three people you would keep from the original list and which three people you would cut. Think of your reasons.

- **Special Guest List 3.** Join another pair of students who have chosen at least two different guests from you and try to convince them to change their minds about their choices. Negotiate a third guest list.

- **Final guest list.** Share your Guest List 3 with the rest of the class, and negotiate a fourth and final guest list.

Video Worksheets

Unit 1: Free coffee!

Before you watch

A. PAIR WORK You are going to watch a video about drivers on Malaysia's highways getting free cups of coffee. Discuss with your partner: What is the reason for giving drivers free coffee? Write a list of possible reasons.

_____

_____

_____

First view

B. Read the questions carefully. Then watch the video and circle the answers.

1. The coffee stop is owned by an international . . .

   coffee company.   tobacco company.   motorway.

2. How many coffee stops are there on Malaysia's north-south highway?

   seventy   seventeen   seven

3. How many cars will travel Malaysia's highways during the holiday period?

   one million   two million   three million

Second view

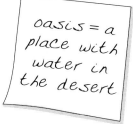

C. Watch the video again and write the missing word in each blank.

REPORTER: Like an oasis, it suddenly appears almost out of _____: a coffee stop. To the sleepy driver, it's protection against dozing off while _____. These days, it seems everyone on Malaysia's motorways is stopping for a cup or _____.

Talk about it

D. GROUP WORK Do you think refreshment stops on highways are a good idea? Why or why not?

Unit 2: Policemen relax.

Before you watch

A. PAIR WORK You are going watch a video about how Indian policemen use music therapy to help them relieve stress. Discuss with your partner: Do you get stressed? Do you ever listen to music to relieve stress? What kind of music?

First view

B. Read the questions carefully. Then watch the video and circle the answers.

1. The music tape is . . .

   two hours long.   one hour long.   less than one hour long.

2. Many officers in the Mumbai police force have high . . .

   injury rates.   cholesterol.   blood pressure.

3. The cassette costs . . .

   eleven dollars.   four dollars.   eleven rupees.

rupee = Indian currency

Second view

C. Watch the video again and write the missing word in each blank.

REPORTER: Many officers in the city have high blood pressure and some have diabetes. Thirty-six or _____ hour shifts are not uncommon. So can the specifically designed rhythms and sounds of Indian and Western classical music really soothe the souls of these _____ officers?

shift = a segment of work time

TRANSLATOR: I feel totally different when I listen to the cassette. My _____ feels transformed.

Talk about it

D. GROUP WORK Do you think having a relaxation session at work is a good idea. Why or why not?

soothe = to calm and relax

Unit 3: Good exercise for seniors

Before you watch

A. PAIR WORK You are going to watch a video about Tai Chi classes for older people. Below are some of the words you are going to hear. Discuss the meaning of these words with your partner.

martial arts   body control   balance   strength   gentle routine

First view

B. Read the questions carefully. Then watch the video and circle the answers.

1. How old is Sarah Young?

   96   106   86

2. Sarah Young thinks Tai Chi is . . .

   wonderful.   beautiful.   tiring.

3. The several-step movement strategy allows people to

   lower their blood pressure.   improve their strength.   regain their balance.

frail = physically weak

Second view

C. Watch the video again and write the missing word in each blank.

DOCTOR: As a geriatrician, that's exactly what we—what we are looking _____. We want people to preserve as much function as they have and not take on excess disabilities.

REPORTER: Researchers say even though Tai Chi is one of the _____ exercises around, seniors interested _____ learning this gentle routine should seek out a class designed for older adults, and they should talk with a doctor before beginning a program.

geriatrician = a doctor specializing in the elderly

Talk about it

D. GROUP WORK Do you think it's a good idea for seniors to do exercise? Why or why not?

Unit 4: Olmec exhibition

Before you watch

A. PAIR WORK You are going to watch a video about an exhibit of Olmec art. Discuss with your partner: what do you know about the Olmec? Write a list of five things that you believe could be true.

_____

_____

_____

First view

B. Read the questions carefully. Then watch the video and circle the answers.

ton = a unit of measurement of weight (approximately)

1. One of the heads in this exhibition weighs . . .

   2 tons.   20 tons.   10 tons.

2. Our main source of information about Olmec society is . . .

   written records.   art objects.   hunting tools.

3. The Olmec believed that the jaguar was an animal spirit who could help . . .

   run the universe.   run a race.   run their country.

Second view

quarry = an open mining site

C. Watch the video again and write the missing word in each blank.

REPORTER: It is the most comprehensive exhibition of Olmec art ever assembled.

MAN: This is the _____ visual culture of the Americas—both continents—and it is a society we know very little about, but to see as much of it as is around us here is, I think, a very thrilling thing.

REPORTER: More than one hundred objects help tell the story of the first people to live in what is now southern Mexico. The Olmec lived in the area three thousand years ago. One thousand years _____, the Aztecs named the region Olman, meaning rubber country, for the rubber trees that surround the area. The Olmec left no written records, but *their* history is written in _____.

Talk about it

D. GROUP WORK Would you have liked to live in the time of the Olmec? Why or why not?

Unit 5: Clean Air

Before you watch

A. PAIR WORK You are going to watch a video about reducing air pollution in New York by setting new standards for vehicles. Below are some of the words about pollution and vehicles that you will hear. Discuss the meaning of these words with your partner.

smog   emissions   tailpipe exhaust   SUV   fuel

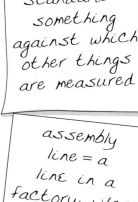

standard = something against which other things are measured

First view

B. Read the questions carefully. Then watch the video and circle the answers.

1. The first state to change its emissions standards was . . .

   California.   New York.   Massachusetts.

2. Vehicles made for New York in the year 2004 must be built so

   emissions are _____ they are in cars sold today.

   the same as   half the amount   more than

3. Having to make two cars, the California model and what the auto

   industry calls the _____ model, is a headache, says one spokesman.

   national   standard   federal

assembly line = a line in a factory, where things are manufactured

Second view

C. Watch the video again and write the missing word in each blank.

impact = effect

REPORTER: Auto makers argue that changing emissions standards will have little impact, without significantly cleaner fuel from the _____ industry, and the changes could add a minimum one hundred dollars to passenger cars and two hundred dollars to _____, a cost most likely picked up by the future buyer. Though old cars won't need to meet the new lower emissions standards, environmentalists still say New York's actions will go a long way to _____ the air we breathe . . . down the road.

Talk about it

D. GROUP WORK Is there a need for stricter emissions standards for vehicles in your country? Why or why not?

Unit 6: When things go wrong . . .

Before you watch

A. PAIR WORK You are going to watch a video that shows the engineers of a space project. The project, to put a Polar Lander vehicle on Mars, cost billions of dollars. Reporters are interviewing the engineers and asking why the project seems to be failing. What could have gone wrong? Write a list of possibilities.

_____

_____

_____

First view

B. Read the questions carefully. Then watch the video and circle the answers.

> *to do the trick = to be successful*

1. After landing, the Mars Polar Lander . . .

   remained silent.   remained immobile.   remained in contact.

2. The news conference followed the _____ attempt to contact the vehicle.

   first   fourth   fifth

3. As time goes by, the engineers are . . .

   more confident.   more confused.   less confident.

> *to fade = to disappear gradually*

Second view

C. Watch the video again and write the missing word in each blank.

REPORTER: High-tech imaging and information from the spacecraft before it _____ Mars' atmosphere indicate the terrain the Lander set down in should have been easy for the vehicle to handle. Reasons why it may not be transmitting range from a _____ glitch to a catastrophe. The engineers have, in a sense, become like doctors trying to revive a dying patient. They are trying everything they can, and they are refusing to give up _____.

> *glitch = a small technical problem*

Talk about it

D. GROUP WORK Do you think governments should spend large amounts of money on space projects? Why or why not?

Unit 7: New York's first youth hostel

Before you watch

A. **PAIR WORK** You are going to watch a video about a youth hostel. With your partner, write down what you think a youth hostel is like and why a youth hostel could be helpful for young travelers.

_____

_____

_____

First view

B. **Read the questions carefully. Then watch the video and circle _T_ for true and _F_ for false.**

1. The new youth hostel is America's largest.   T   F
2. The youth hostel is for international travelers only.   T   F
3. Most American youth hostels are in urban areas.   T   F

> *youth hostel = an inexpensive place to sleep, mainly for young people*

Second view

C. **Watch the video again and write the missing word in each blank.**

REPORTER: They're hoping the hostel brings a sense of life to a community that has had its share of _____ and poverty. Besides that, they say it'll be good for business.

WOMAN: There's dry cleaner's and other kinds of stores in the neighborhood that I know will be providing _____ to the people who stay here, and they're delighted that we're here.

MAN: Apart from being cheap—which makes a big difference if you're traveling on a budget—you actually get to meet an awful lot of people.

REPORTER: And in the city that never _____, there are an awful lot of people to meet.

> *acre = approximately 4,000 meters*

> *bridge a gap = to provide something that is not available*

Talk about it

D. **GROUP WORK** If you could visit New York, would you stay at a youth hostel? Why or why not?

> *dry cleaner's = a business that cleans clothes with cleaning fluid instead of water and detergent*

Unit 8: Innovations in communication

Before you watch

A. PAIR WORK You are going to watch a video about three of the finalists in a competition to invent things to improve communication. Discuss with your partner: What do you think some of these inventions might be? Write a list of three possible inventions.

_____

_____

_____

First view

B. Read the questions carefully. Then watch the video and circle the answers.

1. Bio Control Systems is one of _____ finalists.

   ten   eleven   three

2. The _____ computer controller will help the disabled to use a computer.

   hands-free   free   handy

3. The self-adjusting spectacles will serve the one _____ people who have bad vision.

   thousand   million   billion

> invent =
> to create
> something
> new

> blink =
> to open and
> close the
> eyelids
> rapidly

Second view

C. Watch the video again and write the missing word in each blank.

REPORTER: One of the inventions here is already on the market, and that is the Quicktionary. It's a portable scanner that works as a translator, so, for example, this one _____ from English to Japanese, so all you do is scan the word, wait a couple of seconds, and out comes the word "factory" in Japanese. A second-generation Quicktionary with an audio feature will be _____ next month.

MAN: People will really enjoy using it, umm, the non-native English speakers having to cope with the English environment that they live with on a day in and day out . . .

REPORTER: The winner of the contest will be _____ next month. The grand prize: one hundred thousand dollars.

Talk about it

D. GROUP WORK Which of the three inventions would you award the prize to? Why?

Unit 9: After the flood

Before you watch

A. PAIR WORK You are going to watch a video about helping people after a flood. Discuss with your partner what type of help people affected by a flood will need. Make a list.

_____

_____

_____

First view

B. Read the questions carefully. Then watch the video and circle the answers.

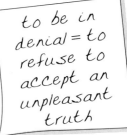

debris = remains of something broken

1. The Veterans Administration bus provides innoculations and basic _____ care.

   flood   disaster   health

2. Because there is so much _____, organisms like E-coli from human waste will be diluted, and they won't pose a serious threat.

   medicine   water   bacteria

evacuee = a person taken away from somewhere because of danger

3. Jim Stankey was working to repair the town's _____ line.

   telephone   electrical   railroad

Second view

C. Watch the video again and write the missing word in each blank.

REPORTER: Not all of the health threats are immediate. Even after the _____ waters recede in the Red River Valley, there'll still be a lot of standing water in some of the fields and neighborhoods, and health officials say they expect there to be a larger than normal mosquito population here this summer. For right now, doctors and _____ counselors keep an eye on evacuees living in shelters trying to fight chronic physical ailments and some new mental stresses like depression and fatigue.

COUNSELOR: We have some people who are in denial. We have a lot of tearful people that are just trying to adjust to this situation.

REPORTER: The Red Cross likens this natural disaster to a _____, and it says it will provide support services for those affected long after the mud is cleared away.

to be in denial = to refuse to accept an unpleasant truth

Talk about it

D. GROUP WORK Would you volunteer to help in a disaster? Why or why not?

Unit 10: Eating after an earthquake

Before you watch

A. PAIR WORK You are going to watch a video about people's eating habits following an earthquake. Below are some words about eating that you will hear. Discuss the meaning of these words with your partner.

appetite   get hungry   overeat   carbohydrate   fast food

First view

B. Read the questions carefully. Then watch the video and circle *T* for true or *F* for false.

1. In stressful situations, the majority of people lose their appetite.   True   False
2. Following the earthquake, sales in fast-food restaurants increased.   True   False
3. The Red Cross provides disaster victims with the right kind of food.   True   False

Second view

haphazard =
without
planning

bingeing =
eating too
much

C. Watch the video again and write the missing word in each blank.

REPORTER: The Red Cross has _____ more than a million meals to the thousands of victims from the January 17ᵗʰ earthquake, many of whom remain in shelters unable to return home. You might think the _____ would cause most people to react like this woman.

WOMAN: Eating habits I've lost a lot—I don't eat as much as I used to. I tend to lose my appetite daily. I don't get as hungry. When I do get hungry, I try to eat but I can't, 'cause my stomach _____.

Talk about it

D. GROUP WORK How do you think you would eat after a natural disaster?

Unit 11: Credit card debt

Before you watch

A. PAIR WORK You are going to watch a video about credit card debt. Why do you think some people get into debt using credit cards? Write a list of possible reasons.

_____

_____

_____

First view

B. Read the questions carefully. Then watch the video and circle the answers.

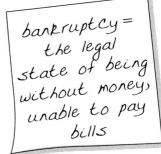

bankruptcy =
the legal
state of being
without money,
unable to pay
bills

1. The woman got into debt, and paying it off was . . .

    easy.   hard.   impossible.

2. Attempts to sign up new customers are having _____ results.

    poor   good   great

3. Consumers have increasingly just said _____ to credit card solicitations.

    yes   no   okay

credit card
limit =
the maximum
amount you
are allowed to
spend on a
credit card

Second view

C. Watch the video again and write the missing word in each blank.

SPEAKER 2: There were about a hundred twelve thousand fewer personal bankrupcies in _____ than in the previous year—the largest one-year decline on record.

REPORTER: Last year's decline is a major break with the _____. Despite the strong economy of recent years, the number of people who filed for bankrupcy in 1998 was still _____ hundred percent higher than two decades earlier.

Talk about it

D. GROUP WORK Do you think using credit cards is good? Why or why not?

Unit 12: It's tme to take a break.

Before you watch

A. PAIR WORK   You are going to watch a video about bargain travel. Below are some of the words you will hear. Discuss the meaning of these words with your partner. If necessary, use a dictionary.

affordable   coupon   package deal   pocketbook

First view

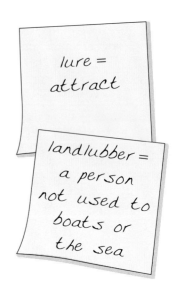

lure =
attract

landlubber =
a person
not used to
boats or
the sea

B. Read the questions carefully. Then watch the video and circle *T* for true and *F* for false.

1. The woman talking about cruises says they are only for the rich.   T   F

2. British Airways offers a package deal with reduced rates for hotels and car rental.   T   F

3. In family-style restaurants, prices are more expensive.   T   F

Second view

C. Watch the video again and write the missing word in each blank.

WOMAN 2: You should always find out what discounts are available to you. If you're a senior citizen, if you're a student _____, if you're a member of a certain organization—let them know that when you're checking into a hotel or when you're _____ transportation.

REPORTER: Many parts of the travel industry are beginning to see brighter days ahead, so it's time to take a break, go out and enjoy _____ surroundings and experience new adventures.

Talk about it

D. GROUP WORK   Which of the travel options suggested in the video would you enjoy? Why?

Vocabulary - Unit 1

Nouns	Adjectives / Adverbs	Verbs	Expressions
a beverage	bitter	attract	A few minutes ago . . .
a brand	expository	brainstorm	As a matter of fact . . .
a club	intensively	compose	I've got to run . . .
concentration	productive	convince	
cream	refreshing	drink	
a disease		guarantee	
a flyer		organize	
literature		recognize	
a milkshake		soothe	
a neighborhood			
origin			
a plantation			
psychology			
a scientist			
a stimulant			

Vocabulary - Unit 2

Nouns	Adjectives / Adverbs	Verbs	Expressions
a boss	addicted to	burn out	get on their case
a confirmation	burnt out	overeat	in control
an expectation	depressed	overbook	lose control
a fair	impatient	overheat	
a journal entry	infamous	oversleep	
a mood	physically	oversped	
the moon	relaxed	overwork	
a newspaper article	stressed out	relax	
a relative	tense		
a scientist	uptight		
stress	work-related		
a website			
a workaholic			

Vocabulary - Unit 3

Nouns	Adjectives / Adverbs	Verbs	Expressions
an adolescent	alive	adopt	Anything wrong?
a carbohydrate	childish	connect	Sorry to hear that.
a caregiver	immature	consume	Oh, no, that's too bad.
a centenarian	per capita	rush	
a companion	rude	suffer	
data	southernmost		
a generation gap	youthful		
an infant			
a lifestyle			
a personality			
a politician			
a senior citizen			
a talk show			
a teenager			
yoga			

Vocabulary - Unit 4

Nouns	Adjectives/ Adverbs	Verbs	Expressions
an artifact	artistic	establish	That isn't my cup of tea.
a biography	kind of	exhibit	
a cathedral	musical	influence	
folk music	occasionally	inspire	
a handicraft			
modern art			
a musician			
pottery			
a sculpture			

Vocabulary - Unit 5

Nouns	Adjectives /Adverbs	Verbs	Expressions
a coast	environmental	breathe in	Forget it!
an engine	powerful	collide	In that case . . .
fuel	sturdy	dump	That's about right.
gasoline	silently	manufacture	
health		occur	
a helicopter		pollute	
a highway		recycle	
a hurricane		reject	
a leaflet		stuck	
a light aircraft			
a manufacturer			
a minivan			
a motorcycle			
a motorist			
an ocean liner			
oil			
a planet			
pollution			
a railway			
a route			
an SUV			
a tire			
traffic			
traffic congestion			
a traffic jam			
a trunk			
a vehicle			
a wreck			

Vocabulary - Unit 6

Nouns	Adjectives /Adverbs	Verbs	Expressions
an argument	accidentally	apologize	Don't worry about it.
a cell phone	deliberately	argue	How could you . . . ?
a laptop	firmly	book	It's just that. . .
a misunderstanding	impatiently	break up	Let's forget about it!
poetry	right	connect to	Right away
a quarrel		lent	
a reconciliation		lose your temper	
a tour			

Vocabulary - Unit 7

Nouns	Adjectives / Adverbs	Verbs	Expressions
abroad	exhausted	fly	Go for it!
a bargain ticket	imaginary	look forward to	I can't make up my mind.
an import tax	lazy	stamp into	(be) on a tight budget
a medical expense	overseas	travel	
a money belt	permanently		
a travel guide	polluted		
travel insurance			
a vaccination			
a visa			

Vocabulary - Unit 8

Nouns	Adjectives / Adverbs	Verbs	Expressions
Braille	long-distance	highlight	Don't even ask.
a chat	once a week	install	. . . in ages
a courier service	on-line		Looks like it.
an emperor			No chance!
a gesture			
instant messaging (IM)			
an interpreter			
a memory			
a romantic			
sign language			
table tennis			
a receipt			
a transaction			

Vocabulary - Unit 9

Nouns	Adjectives / Adverbs	Verbs	Expressions
an aid organization	disastrous	express	Could I have a quick word with you?
a drought	educated		Could we possibly make a time to talk later on?
an earthquake	gently		How would you feel if . . .
emergency services	heart-breaking		I was wondering if we could talk about . . .
famine	high-risk		I'm with you all the way . . .
a firefighter	large-scale		I've been thinking . . .
a flood	man-eating		to keep in touch
a forest fire	poisonous		
a greeting	poverty-stricken		
humor	rapid-response		
medical personnel	world-famous		
a natural disaster			
persecution			
a refugee camp			
a residency			
a risk			
a single-engine airplane			
a training program			
volunteer work			

Vocabulary - Unit 10

Nouns	Adjectives / Adverbs	Verbs	Expressions
an ache	cheerful	accelerate	Don't be silly!
an immune system	emotionally	extend	I think I'll pass.
an injury	hardworking	get better	take better care of
an oven	mentally	heal	to get used to
a posture	retired	sprain	Watch this!

Vocabulary - Unit 11

Nouns	Adjectives / Adverbs	Verbs	Expressions
an account	anonymously	afford	Hold on a minute.
a bank statement	automatically	charge	I can't wait to see that.
a bill	eccentric	inherit	(to be) in debt
currency	foolishly	owe	(to get) into debt
a digital camera	personal	pay off	Keep the change.
an exaggeration	selfish	repay	That's a lot.
an installment	unostentatious	ruin	
privacy	wise		
a psychiatrist			
publicity			
a service charge			
a student loan			
a tax			
a tip			

Vocabulary - Unit 12

Nouns	Adjectives / Adverbs	Verbs	Expressions
admiration	appreciative	confirm	a loved one
baggage	generous	label	For my part . . .
a contribution	imaginative	negotiate	On behalf of . . .
dawn	informative	pay back	
a departure time	lonesome	postpone	
a guest	supportive	put off	
a seaport	trustworthy	stand up for	
a speech	unusual	turn up	
a wedding ring			